More Than Anything

A STUDY ON IDOLATRY

AUBREY COLEMAN

Study Suggestions

We believe that the Bible is true, trustworthy, and timeless, and that it is vitally important for all believers. These study suggestions are intended to help you more effectively study Scripture as you seek to know and love God through His Word.

SUGGESTED STUDY TOOLS

- A Bible

- A double-spaced, printed copy of the Scripture passages that this study covers. You can use a website like *www.biblegateway.com* to copy the text of a passage and print out a double-spaced copy to be able to mark on easily.

- A journal to write notes or prayers

- Pens, colored pencils, and highlighters

- A dictionary to look up unfamiliar words

HOW TO USE THIS STUDY

Begin your study time in prayer. Ask God to reveal Himself to you, to help you understand what you are reading, and to transform you with His Word (Psalm 119:18).

Before you read what is written in each day of the study itself, read the assigned passages of Scripture for that day. Use your double-spaced copy to circle, underline, highlight, draw arrows, and mark in any way you would like to help you dig deeper as you work through a passage.

Read the daily written content provided for the current study day.

Answer the questions that appear at the end of each study day.

The inductive method provides tools for deeper and more intentional Bible study. To study a book of the Bible inductively, work through the steps below after reading background information on the book.

1 OBSERVATION & COMPREHENSION
Key question: What does the text say?

After reading the book of the Bible in its entirety at least once, begin working with smaller portions of the book. Read a passage of Scripture repetitively, and then mark the following items in the text:

- Key or repeated words and ideas
- Key themes
- Transition words (*Ex: therefore, but, because, if/then, likewise, etc.*)
- Lists
- Comparisons & Contrasts
- Commands
- Unfamiliar Words (look these up in a dictionary)
- Questions you have about the text

2 INTERPRETATION
Key question: What does the text mean?

Once you have annotated the text, work through the following steps to help you interpret its meaning:

- Read the passage in other versions for a better understanding of the text.
- Read cross-references to help interpret Scripture with Scripture.
- Paraphrase or summarize the passage to check for understanding.
- Identify how the text reflects the metanarrative of Scripture, which is the story of creation, fall, redemption, and restoration.
- Read trustworthy commentaries if you need further insight into the meaning of the passage.

3 APPLICATION
Key Question: How should the truth of this passage change me?

Bible study is not merely an intellectual pursuit. The truths about God, ourselves, and the gospel that we discover in Scripture should produce transformation in our hearts and lives. Answer the following questions as you consider what you have learned in your study:

- What attributes of God's character are revealed in the passage?

    Consider places where the text directly states the character of God, as well as how His character is revealed through His words and actions.

- What do I learn about myself in light of who God is?

    Consider how you fall short of God's character, how the text reveals your sin nature, and what it says about your new identity in Christ.

- How should this truth change me?

    A passage of Scripture may contain direct commands telling us what to do or warnings about sins to avoid in order to help us grow in holiness. Other times our application flows out of seeing ourselves in light of God's character. As we pray and reflect on how God is calling us to change in light of His Word, we should be asking questions like, "How should I pray for God to change my heart?" and "What practical steps can I take toward cultivating habits of holiness?"

ATTRIBUTES OF GOD

ETERNAL

God has no beginning and
no end. He always was,
always is, and always will be.

HAB 1:12 / REV. 1:8 / IS. 41:4

FAITHFUL

God is incapable of
anything but fidelity.
He is loyally devoted to
His plan and purpose.

2 TIM. 2:13 / DEUT. 7:9
HEB. 10:23

GLORIOUS

God is ultimately
beautiful, deserving of
all praise and honor.

REV. 19:1 / PS. 104:1
EX. 40:34-35

GOOD

God is pure; there is no
defilement in Him.
He is unable to sin, and
all He does is good.

GEN. 1:31 / PS. 34:8 / PS. 107:1

GRACIOUS

God is kind, giving to us
gifts and benefits which
we are undeserving of.

2 KINGS 13:23 / PS. 145:8
IS. 30:18

HOLY

God is undefiled and
unable to be in the presence
of defilement. He is
sacred and set-apart.

REV. 4:8 / LEV. 19:2 / HAB. 1:13

IMMUTABLE

God does not change.
He is the same yesterday,
today, and tomorrow.

1 SAM. 15:29 / ROM. 11:29
JAMES 1:17

JEALOUS

God is desirous of receiving
the praise and affection
He rightly deserves.

EX. 20:5 / DEUT. 4:23-24
JOSH. 24:19

JUST

God governs in
perfect justice. He acts in
accordance with justice.
In Him there is no
wrongdoing or dishonesty.

IS. 61:8 / DEUT. 32:4 / PS. 146:7-9

LOVE

God is eternally, enduringly,
steadfastly loving and
affectionate. He does not
forsake or betray His
covenant love.

JN. 3:16 / EPH. 2:4-5 / 1 JN. 4:16

MERCIFUL

God is compassionate,
withholding us from
the wrath that we are
deserving of.

TITUS 3:5 / PS. 25:10
LAM. 3:22-23

OMNIPOTENT

God is all-powerful;
His strength is unlimited.

MAT. 19:26 / JOB 42:1-2
JER. 32:27

OMNIPRESENT

God is everywhere; His
presence is near and
permeating.

PROV. 15:3 / PS. 139:7-10
JER. 23:23-24

OMNISCIENT

God is all-knowing;
there is nothing
unknown to Him.

PS. 147:4 / I JN. 3:20
HEB. 4:13

PATIENT

God is long-suffering and
enduring. He gives ample
opportunity for people to
turn toward Him.

ROM. 2:4 / 2 PET. 3:9 / PS. 86:15

RIGHTEOUS

God is blameless and
upright. There is no
wrong found in Him.

PS. 119:137 / JER. 12:1
REV. 15:3

SOVEREIGN

God governs over all things;
He is in complete control.

COL. 1:17 / PS. 24:1-2
1 CHRON. 29:11-12

TRUE

God is our measurement
of what is fact. By Him
are we able to discern
true and false.

JN. 3:33 / ROM. 1:25 / JN. 14:6

WISE

God is infinitely
knowledgeable and is
judicious with His
knowledge.

IS. 46:9-10 / IS. 55:9 / PROV. 3:19

Creation

In the beginning, God created the universe. He made the world and everything in it. He created humans in His own image to be His representatives on the earth.

Fall

The first humans, Adam and Eve, disobeyed God by eating from the fruit of the Tree of Knowledge of Good and Evil. Because of sin, the world was cursed. The punishment for sin is death, and because of Adam's original sin, all humans are sinful and condemned to death.

Redemption

God sent his Son to become a human and redeem His people. Jesus Christ lived a sinless life but died on the cross to pay the penalty for sin. He resurrected from the dead and ascended into heaven. All who put their faith in Jesus are saved from death and freely receive the gift of eternal life.

Restoration

One day, Jesus Christ will return again and restore all that sin destroyed. He will usher in a new heaven and new earth where all who trust in Him will live eternally with glorified bodies in the presence of God.

Table of Contents

WEEK 1
/
DAY 1

"

GOD IS THE ONLY
ONE WHO CAN
fulfill & satisfy
OUR EVERY LONGING.

"

BIBLICAL UNDERSTANDING OF IDOLATRY

Biblical Understanding of Idolatry

READ EXODUS 20:3-6, PSALM 135:15-18, JONAH 2:8, ROMANS 1:25

When God created man and woman, He crafted them with hearts to worship Him alone. He did so with intentions of drawing near to His people in a loving relationship and dwelling with them. The only reasonable response from Adam and Eve should have been awe and adoration of Him. They had everything they needed. Yet, when confronted with temptation, Adam and Eve chose to believe a lie. They chose to believe that God was not enough and that He was withholding good from them. Adam and Eve chose to believe that they could create better gods for themselves. Their response to God's gracious love and provision became misplaced worship. The misplaced worship of mankind ultimately led to the entrance of sin into the world and broken relationship with God. From that moment on, God's people were tempted to misplace their worship in a number of ways. We experience this same temptation today. We are tempted to believe that God is not enough and that we need something more. When we misdirect our worship toward anything other than God, it is called idolatry.

When God created man and woman, He crafted them with hearts to worship Him alone.

The most prevalent form of idolatry in the Old Testament was the worship of images, or figures, that were intended to represent various pagan deities. An example of this is found in Exodus 32 after God used Moses to lead the Israelites out of slavery from Egypt. When they reached Mount Sinai, Moses went up the mountain to hear from the Lord. While he was there, the Israelites grew impatient and tired of waiting for him to come down. After all that God had accomplished to save them from the hands of the Egyptians, the Israelites doubted Him and decided to make a physical idol as they had seen in Egypt. They took gold and turned it into a golden calf to worship. They worshiped and made sacrifices to the calf, presenting their reverence and adoration for it. Their impatience with God led them to create a god for themselves. Even after all God had done to rescue and care for them, they forsook Him and turned to worthless idols.

Though the Israelites worshiped idols outwardly, the Bible is clear that idolatry begins in the heart. Idolatry is essentially setting something or someone other than God upon the throne of our hearts. The Israelites redirected the affections in their hearts well before they built and exalted the golden calf. Ezekiel 14 sheds light on the reality that idols begin in the heart. In the third verse, God says to Ezekiel that certain elders of Israel have "set up idols in their hearts" and have placed "sinful stumbling blocks in front of themselves." Even if they outwardly seemed faithful in their worship, their hearts revealed worship of false gods. God sends out a warning in verse 4 as He explains that when anyone "sets up idols in his heart and puts his sinful stumbling block in front of himself… I, the Lord, will answer him appropriately. I will answer him according to His many idols…" God is looking at the condition of the heart. He is not only looking at the outward displays of worship but the true, inward devotion and affections as well.

The pages of the Bible showcase the sin of idolatry in various forms, from worshiping forged images, to worshiping wealth and possessions, to worshiping passions, power, and desires of the flesh. As Christians today, we may or may not find ourselves creating physical idols, but there are many other things we can be tempted to idolize. These can be anything leading us to place our worship elsewhere. God made His commandment clear in Exodus 20:3 — "Do not have other gods besides me, do not make an idol for yourself, whether in the shape of anything in the heavens above or on the earth below or in the waters under the earth." Idolatry is sin. It is exalting anything that is not God. Idolatry is born out of the lie that says God is not enough for us. It misleads us to believe that we can make better gods for ourselves.

Even as God's people turned away from Him, the truth of His character is that He continually and graciously pursues His people. He offers forgiveness freely to all who repent, turn to Him, and therefore, dethrone their idols. As we look to God's Word, we are reminded time and time again that God is the only one who can fulfill and satisfy our every longing. He is the only one who can make and keep His promises. He is the only one who can meet our every need. No pursuit, pleasure, or person will ever make a comparable god. Not only does our faithful worship of God glorify Him, but it is also for our greatest good. Through God's covenant promise, bound by love and sacrifice, He promises to be with His people and to never leave or forsake them. No idol can uphold such a promise. God relentlessly pursues His people, even when they forget or dishonor Him. God makes this tangibly clear for us by sending His Son to save us from our sin and reconcile us back to Himself. As we are tempted and tried by distractions that try to tell us otherwise, we must return again and again to His Word to be reminded of what is true. As the Spirit reveals the idols of our hearts, may we be quick to repent and run to the One who deserves our full awe and worship.

The idols that vie for our worship look different for every Christian. Often, we may not be able to identify them on our own. Over the course of this study, we will take an in-depth look at specific things we may be tempted to turn into idols. We will ask ourselves hard questions. Where does my heart turn to find fulfillment and satisfaction? Where do I seek purpose? Where do I seek security? Does this consume my thoughts? Does this control my decisions? What tempts me to believe that God is not enough? The hope and goal of this study is to unveil anything that may lead us to misdirect our worship to something other than God. He is the only one worthy of our deepest affection and devotion. As we dive into this five week study, may our hearts ultimately be shaped by the biblical truths we uncover to love God more than anything else.

WHAT IS YOUR BIBLICAL UNDERSTANDING OF IDOLATRY?

PREPARING FOR THIS STUDY, CONSIDER WHAT IDOLS VIE FOR
YOUR WORSHIP. WHERE DOES YOUR HEART TURN TO FIND FULFILLMENT,
PURPOSE, SECURITY, OR SATISFACTION?

AS YOU BEGIN THIS STUDY, WRITE A PRAYER ASKING GOD TO OPEN YOUR
EYES TO SEE ANY IDOLATROUS WAY IN YOUR HEART.

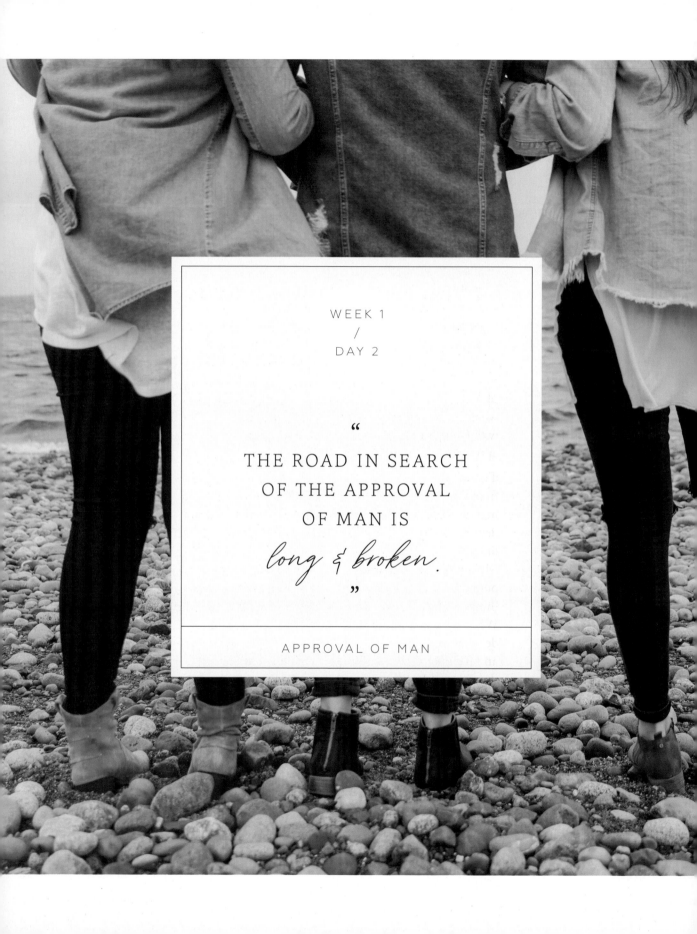

WEEK 1
/
DAY 2

"

THE ROAD IN SEARCH
OF THE APPROVAL
OF MAN IS

long & broken.

"

APPROVAL OF MAN

Approval of Man

READ GALATIANS 1:10, JOHN 12:43,
COLOSSIANS 3:23-24

Many of us enjoy the accepting words of someone dear, a thumbs up for a job well done, or a confirming response for our efforts. It makes us feel good, supported, and acknowledged by those whose opinions we most value. The approval of others can encourage and affirm us in our efforts. It is a kind word and a generous way of showing support. To be affirmed is a natural desire and part of being human. In fact, the desire for approval, in and of itself, is not a bad thing. God the Father affirmed his Son at His baptism with resounding words of approval: "This is my beloved Son, with whom I am well pleased" (Matthew 3:17). And there is a day coming for all of God's people when He has promised to fully and finally approve all who have been united with Christ in His life, death, and resurrection. So, how is it that the desire for approval can potentially become an idol in our lives?

Though the desire for approval itself is not sin, it is who we long to receive it from that leads us into sin. It is when we search for the praise that comes from man and not the praise that comes from God. It is when our performance is dependent on what others think and how they will respond. Many of us may find this to be something we wrestle with. We can identify approval as an idol when it begins to rule our hearts and minds. We see it clearly when we are bound by what others think about us. This can shape the way we live, the things we buy, the way we look, the way we think, and the way we interact. When we crave approval, we may be willing to compromise too much in order that we do not disappoint someone. We might say yes to too many things and fill up our schedules in fear of disappointing someone. We may avoid sharing our thoughts and opinions in fear they will contradict with someone else's. We may fear the judgment of others and loosen up our convictions in order to gain their approval.

We can identify approval as an idol when it begins to rule our hearts and minds.

The road in search of the approval of man is long and broken. It becomes an endless cycle of living to please others. Even if temporarily satisfying, it will never lead us to a place of hope and fulfillment. It will always leave us searching for more, and we will likely lose ourselves in the process. But more so, it will lead us in pursuit of something that cannot ever be attained. We cannot be fully approved by man. Mankind does not have the power to do so, and the pursuit is in vain. When we place such an expectation on another sinful, limited person, that person will always fail us. He or she cannot possibly bear the weight of our desire for approval. The only One with the true power to approve us once and for all is God. He has offered us full and final validation and acceptance through the sacrifice of His Son, Jesus Christ. No man can offer this to us. It is only through Jesus' life, death, and resurrection that we can stand before a holy God as one approved.

Turning from the idol of approval looks like holding the affirmations of others loosely and holding fast to the truth of Scripture. We will not feel the need to depend on others to approve of us. Instead, we will find ourselves anchored in the approval of Jesus. This allows us to receive encouragement as a gift. Yet it also keeps us from being crushed when we do not receive it. It helps relieve the pressure of expectations we place on others to provide it for us. When we put our faith and hope in Jesus as our ultimate Savior, we can stand confidently before God and others, approved like His own Son. God's approval is not temporary or dependent on our performance and circumstances but is rooted in the finished work of Jesus. May this glorious truth set us free from idolizing the approval of others and stir our hearts in worship of the only One who can offer us true approval.

God's approval is not temporary or dependent on our performance and circumstances but is rooted in the finished work of Jesus.

HOW DOES THE APPROVAL OF MAN AFFECT THE WAY YOU LIVE? HOW ARE
YOU AFFECTED BY A LACK OF APPROVAL FROM OTHERS?

HOW DOES THE APPROVAL OF GOD IN CHRIST COMPARE TO THE APPROVAL OF MAN?

IN WHAT WAYS HAVE THE EXPECTATIONS OF APPROVAL FROM OTHERS
AFFECTED YOUR RELATIONSHIPS?

WHAT DOES IT LOOK LIKE TO TURN FROM THE IDOL OF APPROVAL?

WEEK 1
/
DAY 3

"

WE NEED

the help of Jesus

TO CARRY US

THROUGH EACH DAY.

"

BUSYNESS

Busyness

READ LUKE 10:38-42, EPHESIANS 5:15-17

Do you have those moments when you are glancing at the clock, counting the seconds, and waiting for one appointment to end so that you can make it to the next? The time in between is a sprint to the car, a quick phone call, and a moment to breathe. But by the end of the day, you are exhausted, wondering where the time went and why the day felt like a race. Do moments like this happen often? Do you schedule your days from start to finish? Are you constantly looking for something to do and some way to keep yourself busy? Do you task and schedule yourself to the point of exhaustion every day? Do you find yourself pushing God to the margins of your calendar? If you answered yes to most of these questions, you may be tempted to idolize busyness.

If we look at the amount of things we can do and accomplish in a day as a measure of worth and value, it has become an idol.

In a fast-paced culture, it is easy to fall into the trap of busyness. But the pursuit of busyness is not just limited to today's culture. The Bible addresses this very temptation. In Luke 10, Martha and her sister, Mary, welcomed Jesus into their home. Martha began busying herself with many tasks, while Mary sat and listened to Jesus speak. Martha grew agitated that her sister was not helping with the many tasks, but Jesus reminded her of what is most important: "Martha, Martha, you are worried and upset about many things, but one thing is necessary. Mary has made the right choice, and it will not be taken away from her" (Luke 10:41-42). Martha felt it was more valuable to busy herself with service, even if it was taking away from what Jesus truly desired of her—spending time with Him. Jesus makes clear the value that each of the women's actions held. Though Martha's intentions were likely well meaning, she was busying herself with the wrong things. She was more devoted to her own tasks than to what the Lord was asking of her. We can identify busyness as an idol in our lives by asking ourselves if these same things are true for us. Even if we do not enjoy being busy or delight in full schedules, there are indicators that reveal to us that our hearts are clinging to it for worth and value. If we look at the amount of things we can do and accomplish in a day as a measure of worth and value, it has become an idol. If we find that our days are ruled and restricted by deadlines and time restraints, it has become an idol. If we are unable to relinquish our schedules, tasks, and plans to the Lord, it has become an idol.

Like many things, being busy does not always turn idolatrous. There is a time and place to be busy with the Lord's work. We see this visibly in the life and ministry of Jesus. He traveled, taught the Scriptures, spoke the truth of God, discipled men, ate with friends and strangers, served the community, and used every opportunity to incorporate the good news of the gospel. I imagine His days were long and full. But Jesus' busy schedule served kingdom purposes and was solely dependent on what the Father asked of Him. Jesus never allowed the busyness of His ministry to take the throne of His heart. Instead, He was always in service to the Lord. We must be discerning with how we use our time and fill our days, even in doing the Lord's work, so that we remain alert to the temptation of falling victim to spiritual busyness.

You may feel you are in a particularly busy season of life. You may even feel you have young children and their schedules to accommodate. Maybe your job is extremely demanding. Maybe you are caring for an aging parent. Maybe you are wearing a few too many hats. In any case, Jesus models perfectly how, through prayer and rest, we can resist the temptation to idolize our busy schedules. One thing we see frequently in the ministry of Jesus is that He pulled away from the crowds—even from His disciples—to spend time alone with God in prayer. Prayer leads us to reorient our heart and attention toward God. It brings His work to the forefront of our days over our own. Spending time in prayer gives us opportunities to slow down and take ourselves out of our self-consumed schedules. It provides the opportunity to ask God what He would desire for us to accomplish each day and to fill our schedules with things that are honoring and glorifying to Him. Another thing we see in the ministry of Jesus is that He intentionally modeled rest for us. He took time to stop and refuel. We are limited in our physical bodies, and we cannot power through on our own strength. Our bodies grow tired and weary when our days are full. We physically and mentally need rest. Therefore, it is necessary for us to take time in our days to slow down and rest. This may look differently in every stage of life, yet it serves as a necessary reminder that we cannot do it all. We need the help of Jesus to carry us through each day.

As we identify the temptation to busy our days, may the Word of God remind us that our days are not our own but belong to God and His work. We are called according to God's purposes and not our own. So we must wisely and prayerfully consider how we should use our time. We must relinquish our busy schedules time and time again to the Lord. But as we do, may we be comforted by the truth that God works all things for the good of His people and for the glory of His name. May we redirect our worship from busy days to the One who truly rules our days.

Jesus models perfectly how, through prayer and rest, we can resist the temptation to idolize our busy schedules.

QUESTIONS

HOW DOES BUSYNESS AFFECT THE WAY YOU LIVE?
HOW ARE YOU AFFECTED BY AN EMPTY SCHEDULE OR IDLE TIME?

HOW CAN YOU RELATE WITH THE STORY OF MARY AND MARTHA
IN REGARD TO BUSYNESS?

IN WHAT WAYS DOES THE MINISTRY OF JESUS REVEAL A DIFFERENCE IN BEING
BUSY WITH YOUR OWN WORK AND BEING BUSY WITH THE LORD'S WORK?

WHAT DOES IT LOOK LIKE TO TURN FROM THE IDOL OF BUSYNESS?

WEEK 1
/
DAY 4

"

GOD CAN USE ANY
OPPORTUNITY TO MAKE US

trust & rely

ON HIM MORE.

"

CONTROL

Control

READ JEREMIAH 17:5-8, EPHESIANS 1:20-23

We are surrounded by things we cannot control—a medical diagnosis, natural disasters, flat tires, and lost luggage. There is not a minute that passes that something is not out of our control. We see evidence of this simply by watching the temperature rise and fall each day from no contribution of our own. Take a moment to consider all the things that have happened today that have fallen outside of the realm of your control.

There is not a minute that passes that something is not out of our control.

Even with each of these examples, the desire to control remains a temptation for many of us in our lives. When we desire to control, we want everything to go according to our plans, and we depend on ourselves to keep everything in order. We may be uncomfortable with the unknown and the unpredictable, and therefore, we grip tightly to that which we want to keep safe and secure in our lives. There is wisdom in being cautious, prepared, and thoughtful about our circumstances. Proverbs 21:5 tells us, "The plans of the diligent certainly lead to profit, but anyone who is reckless certainly becomes poor." However, we must ultimately trust in the Lord for the outcome of our plans and depend fully on His sovereign control in every circumstance. The inclination to control can turn to idolatry when we hold tightly to our desired plans and outcomes. It becomes an idol when the absence of control leads us to sin. The idol of control promises that nothing can happen outside of our perfect planning, preparation, and precautions. It promises that we can establish our own steps. It promises that we do not have to be afraid because we have checked off every box. But the idol of control will never keep those promises.

Consider the story of Sarah in Genesis 16. God promised a son to her and her husband, Abraham, but as time passed and Sarah was unable to conceive, she grew impatient with God. She decided to take matters into her own hands. She had a servant named Hagar, and she asked Hagar to bear a son with Abraham so the promise would be fulfilled. Hagar obeyed and conceived and gave birth to a son named Ishmael. As a result, Sarah blamed Abraham for the suffering she felt and began to mistreat and shame Hagar. She eventually threw her out of her home. Sarah's initial aim was to control her circumstances so that she could fulfill God's promise to her. She had grown impatient with God's timing and doubted God would follow through with His promise. The result was not that God's plan was thwarted but that Sarah suffered the consequences of doubting God and trusting in herself, instead. Fortunately for Sarah, God fulfilled His promise to her. We see the fruit of this promise in Genesis 21 when Sarah gives birth to her son, Isaac.

What we learn from this example is that our interventions and manipulations to exert control over our circumstances do not change God's plans and promises. But when we idolize control to the extent of sinning, we will experience the consequences. We might lose our temper, take it out on those around us, invoke anxiety, or blame others. These are only a few examples of how this idol can lead us into further sin. Ultimately, we will find that our desire to control will never be enough to alter or dictate our circumstances. Instead, in our failed attempts, we have the opportunity to remember that God is more capable and more trustworthy to handle our circumstances than we are.

God's power and sufficiency are displayed perfectly in Christ. Nothing happens outside of His rule and reign. We can trust fully in God's plan and purpose because we know He can actually bring them to be. We can rely fully on God's promises because we know He can actually fulfill them. He is good and does good, therefore every way that He shapes and purposes our plans is ultimately for our good. He is far more capable of seeing what is best for us than we are. As we identify the desire to control as an idol in our life, we must continually repent of our misplaced worship and relinquish our plans and expectations to the Lord. When we come to God, confessing our lack of control and desire to trust fully in Him, He is eager and willing to receive us. Just as He comforted Sarah in her distress, so He will also comfort His people. Even when we are faithless, God remains faithful (2 Timothy 2:13). God can use any opportunity to make us trust and rely on Him more. Each opportunity develops a greater understanding that in all things, we must loosen our grip on control and hold fast to the faithfulness of Jesus.

We can trust fully in God's plan and purpose because we know
He can actually bring them to be.

WHAT IS THE IDOL OF CONTROL? IN WHAT WAYS MIGHT YOU BE
TEMPTED TO IDOLIZE CONTROL?

READ JEREMIAH 17:5-8. HOW DOES THIS PASSAGE COMPARE TRUSTING IN OURSELVES
TO TRUSTING IN THE LORD? IN WHAT WAYS DOES THIS PASSAGE HELP YOU FIGHT
AGAINST THE DESIRE TO TAKE CONTROL AND TRUST IN YOURSELF?

WHAT DOES IT LOOK LIKE TO REPENT OF AND RELINQUISH
CONTROL IN YOUR OWN LIFE?

WEEK 1
/
DAY 5

"

THE TRUTH ABOUT ANYTHING
THAT PROMISES TO
bring us comfort
OUTSIDE OF JESUS IS
THAT IT WILL NOT LAST.
"

COMFORT

Comfort

READ LUKE 9:57-62, 2 CORINTHIANS 1:3-7

An idol today that lures and tempts in the most subtle and discreet way is the idol of comfort. For many, the expectation of running water, a stocked fridge, reliable transportation, and a warm bed are typical comforts. But we may run to more things like a beautiful home, a healthy family, two-day Amazon shipping, coffee shop lattes, and frequent travels. We are provided many opportunities to be comfortable even though that looks different for every Christian. Comforts are gifts given by God to be enjoyed and utilized, intended to lead us to praise and thank Him. But when those comforts are taken away, can we still praise and thank God? Can we remain faithful even in the midst of discomfort?

Comforts are gifts given by God to be enjoyed and utilized, intended to lead us to praise and thank Him.

Worldly comforts can be easily accessible, and we may be tempted to buy into the lie that we deserve to be comfortable. However, the Bible never promises an easy and comfortable life for the Christian. In fact, Jesus tells us we will have trouble in this world (John 16:33). He is speaking out of experience. During his earthly ministry, Jesus did not have an outstanding appearance (Isaiah 53:2), great financial and material security (Luke 9:3), and often not a place to lay his head at night (Luke 9:58). Even beyond the expected comforts, Jesus was mocked, ridiculed, persecuted, and eventually put to death. He makes it clear that the cost of faithfulness is high. He tells His disciples that if anyone wants to follow Him, they must deny themselves, take up their cross, and follow Him (Matthew 16:24).

Denying ourselves means denying our expected earthly comforts and possessions, denying our assumed amenities and easy ways of life, and denying acceptance from the ways of the world. If we are unable to relinquish the comforts of this world, we grow in a conditional means of following Jesus. Practically we live in a way that says, "I will follow you, as long as I can still (fill in the blank)." When our comforts are leveraged, our affections become less directed toward Jesus and more directed toward whatever is maintaining our comfort levels. If we are willing to do anything to keep those comforts, it has become an idol. If we are unwilling to follow Jesus in order to keep those comforts, it has become an idol.

The truth about anything that promises to bring us comfort outside of Jesus is that it will not last. It will eventually fail and disappoint us. And it certainly will not sustain or save us. Even in our best efforts, we cannot comfort ourselves with the things of this world. When faced with trial, grief, and suffering, no amount of earthly comforts will bring us the hope that we crave. Our tears are not dried by the remembrance of our air-conditioned homes. Our hearts are not mended by internet access. Our sorrows are not consoled by our favorite vacation destinations. Even if they bring temporal relief, they will never bring us lasting comfort.

The Bible does not shy away from speaking about the discomfort that comes with the Christian life. However, it does not leave us there. We are promised a true comforter. The only true comfort of this world lies in the open and inviting arms of Jesus who says, "Come to me" (Matthew 11:28). He provides consolation, healing, and hope that we search endlessly for to relieve our burdens, and He offers it freely and generously when we come to Him. When disparities and discomforts of this world arise, Jesus promises a day when there will be no more tears, no more pain, and no more death (Revelation 21:4). They will be gone forever. He is the only one who can make and fulfill this promise to us. So as we are tempted and tried by the things of this world to be comforted, may we turn from this idol by looking to Christ for true shelter and solace.

When faced with trial, grief, and suffering, no amount of earthly comforts will bring us the hope that we crave.

IN WHAT WAYS ARE YOU TEMPTED TO IDOLIZE THE COMFORTS OF THIS WORLD?
HAVE YOU EVER HELD SO TIGHTLY TO BEING COMFORTABLE THAT IT
LED YOU TO DISOBEY GOD?

READ LUKE 9:57-62. WHAT ARE THINGS THAT MAY TEMPT YOU TO TURN BACK AS
YOU FOLLOW JESUS? ARE YOU EVER TEMPTED TO SAY, "I WILL FOLLOW JESUS,
AS LONG AS I CAN STILL (FILL IN THE BLANK)?" WHAT DO YOU FILL IN THE BLANK?

HOW DOES GODLY COMFORT DIFFER FROM WORLDLY COMFORT?
WHERE DOES OUR TRUE HOPE FOR COMFORT LIE?

MEDITATE ON PSALM 23. PRAY AND ASK GOD TO TURN TO HIM
AS OUR TRUE COMFORTER.

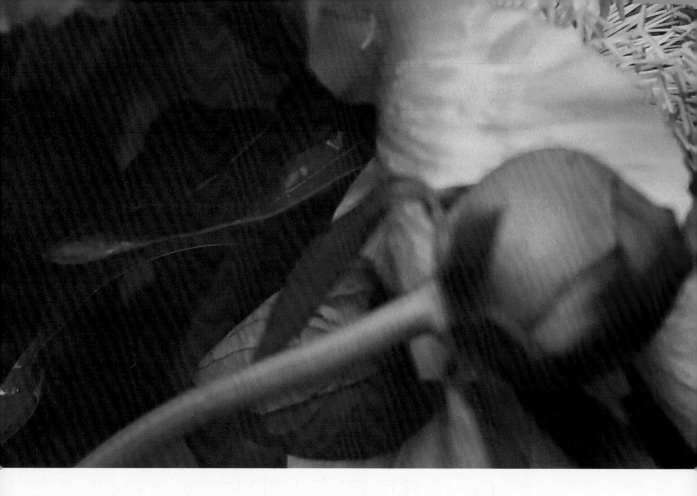

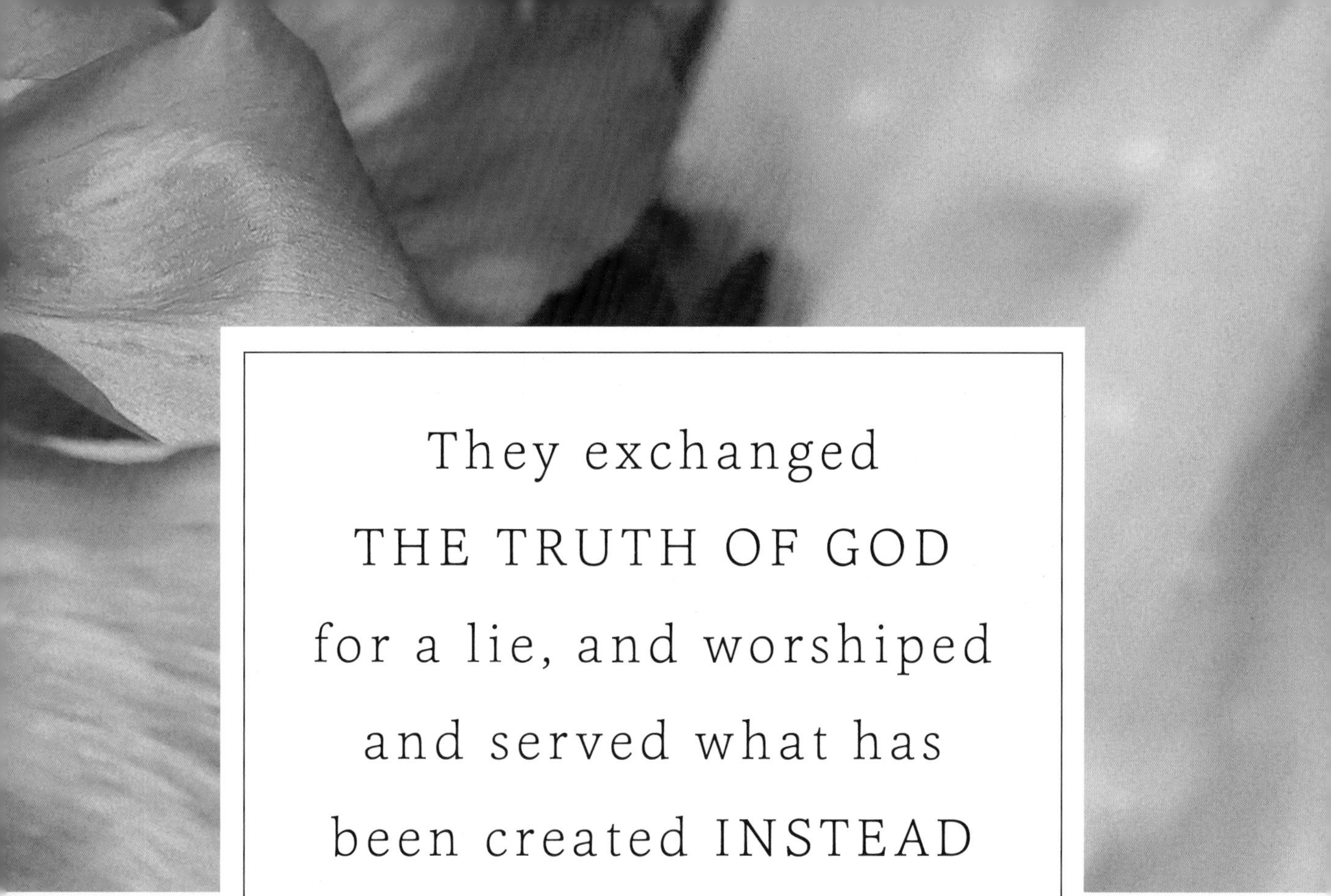

They exchanged
THE TRUTH OF GOD
for a lie, and worshiped
and served what has
been created INSTEAD
OF THE CREATOR,
who is praised forever.
Amen.

Romans 1:25

WEEK 1 SCRIPTURE MEMORY

Week One Reflection

review all passages from this week

Paraphrase the passages that stood out to you the most this week.

_____

_____

_____

_____

_____

_____

_____

_____

_____

What did you observe from this week's text about God and His character?	What do these passages teach about the condition of mankind and about yourself?
_____	_____
_____	_____
_____	_____
_____	_____
_____	_____
_____	_____
_____	_____
_____	_____

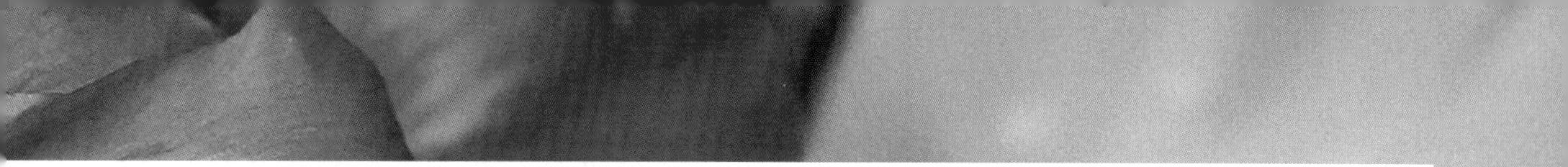

How do these passages point to the gospel?

_____

_____

_____

_____

_____

_____

How should you respond to these passages? What is the personal application?

_____

_____

_____

_____

_____

_____

What specific action steps can you take this week to apply these passages?

WEEK 2
/
DAY 1

"

THE TRUTH

of the gospel

REVEALS THAT WE ARE

NOT ENOUGH, BUT

JESUS CHRIST IS.

"

SELF-SUFFICIENCY

Self-Sufficiency

READ JOHN 15:1-11, 2 CORINTHIANS 12:9-10

Cultural mantras fuel the fire of self-sufficiency by chanting, "You are enough!" We see it all over social media, highlighted in books, coined as a slogan for numerous brands, and emphasized by motivational speakers. This mantra, at the roots, is to preach self-help, self-care, and self-sufficiency. At first glance, these claims seem empowering and emboldening, but they lead to the exhausting pursuit of building our lives solely around ourselves, our own strength, and our own sufficiency. It aims to build us up in a way that actually pushes God and others out. Ultimately, it feeds the lie that we only need ourselves.

The idol of self-sufficiency reveals itself when our confidence rests solely in ourselves. This can look a number of ways. We may struggle with vulnerability and not wanting to show any sign of weakness. We might grow slow to repent by thinking we can just modify our behavior and do better next time. We might read our Bibles less, thinking we have already read through it enough and memorized enough. We might struggle to receive critique and feedback, seeing little of our weaknesses and imperfections. We might even avoid asking others for help in order to appear as if we have everything under control. We may experience burn out more frequently in our relationships, careers, and ministry efforts, because we depend only on ourselves. The greater danger of this idol is that it preaches a life that revolves around us and our efforts and ultimately can lead to a daily denial of our need for Jesus.

The idol of self-sufficiency reveals itself when our confidence rests solely in ourselves.

The gospel preaches the opposite of self-sufficiency. For the Christian, we come to understand the gospel when we understand our great need for a Savior. The hope of Jesus rings loud and clear when we find ourselves at the depths of our depleted efforts to save ourselves. Maybe we grow exhausted from our efforts to appear righteous, or maybe we find ourselves in a hole of sin we cannot escape. In either scenario, the truth of the gospel reveals that we are not enough, but Jesus Christ is. This is good and glorious news to us. We are not being asked to pull ourselves up by our bootstraps to attain our own righteousness. Instead, Romans 10:9 says, "If you confess with your mouth, 'Jesus is Lord,' and believe in your heart that God raised him from the dead, you will be saved." Christ is sufficient for us. By looking to ourselves, we will always come up short, but Jesus Christ offers us the fullest and most abundant hope in Himself.

The Bible shines with the sufficiency of Jesus. We see an example of this in John 15. Jesus says that He is the vine, and we are the branches. If we remain in Him, we produce much fruit, but apart from Him we can do nothing. He is the all-sufficient source! Nothing happens apart from Him. We turn from the idol of self-sufficiency by acknowledging our weakness to God and others often. Asking for help and recognizing our limitations are a couple of tangible ways we live this out. When we are able to humble ourselves in such a way, we gain access to the grace and sufficiency of Jesus who says, "my power is perfected in weakness" (2 Corinthians 12:9). We are able to experience the unlimited nature of God and draw from His strength over our own.

As we are tempted to buy into the self-sufficiency idol, may we ask God to bring us to our knees to remind us of our inadequacies. May we abide in God's Word to daily remind us of our unfailing need for Him. And may we continually preach the gospel to ourselves, remembering that we are not enough on our own. Implanting this truth frees us to turn from ourselves and cling to the sufficiency of Christ. In Him, we are more than enough.

May we abide in God's Word to daily remind us of our unfailing need for Him.

IN WHAT WAYS ARE YOU TEMPTED TO CLING TO THE SELF-SUFFICIENCY IDOL?

HOW DOES THIS IDOL AFFECT YOUR RELATIONSHIP WITH GOD AND OTHERS?

HOW DOES THE GOSPEL FREE YOU FROM THE NEED TO BE SUFFICIENT
ON YOUR OWN?

WEEK 2
/
DAY 2

"

THERE IS NO APPEARANCE
MORE VALUABLE
THAN THAT OF

heirs with Jesus Christ.

"

APPEARANCE

Appearance

READ COLOSSIANS 3:1-17, PHILIPPIANS 1:20

Much of our lives is displayed through the perspective of the outside looking in. Many will make judgments and perceptions about the way we live, merely based on what they can tangibly see. Our appearance can refer to the way we dress, the way we decorate, the way our marriage looks, the way our parenting looks, the way our jobs look, the way our ministry looks, or anything that we display externally in our lives. The thing about appearance though is that it is not always what it seems to be. Appearance can be altered, manipulated, or crafted in a way that leads others to believe something about us that may or may not be true.

We all present ourselves in some way to a watching world. However, we need to ask ourselves questions as we consider our appearance. Does my appearance honor God? Is my pursuit of appearance leading me to sin? These questions get to the heart of the matter. There are numerous ways the pursuit of appearance can look in the life of a Christian. A college student may wear only high-end clothes and accessories to appear to others that she has wealth and fortune. A married couple may present their relationship to be happy and healthy when they are struggling with hardship and difficulty behind closed doors. A friend may be kind to others in person yet gossip about them behind their backs. A ministry leader may be faithfully serving in the church but be neglecting his family at home.

When we are unable to present ourselves honestly and honorably, at the cost of keeping up our appearance, it has become an idol.

Keeping up appearance is not something new. In the New Testament, the Pharisees, the religious leaders of the day, would honor God with their lips but dishonor Him in their hearts. Their outward appearance seemed one way but served as a false depiction of what they were believing in their hearts. When we are unable to present ourselves honestly and honorably, at the cost of keeping up our appearance, it has become an idol. If we have become hypocritical or deceptive in the way we present ourselves to others, it has become an idol. A true mark of anything becoming idolatrous in our lives is whether we are willing to sin in order to keep it. If we are unwilling to relinquish our appearance at the cost of falling into sin, idolatry is born.

Though appearance may be able to fool the perspective of the world, God is never fooled. He looks beyond our appearance into the reality of our hearts. This does not mean that we should not care about how we present ourselves to others. There is a good and godly way to care about our appearance. Scripture reminds us that we are representatives of Christ, called to reflect Him with our lives to a watching world. We are called to conduct ourselves in a manner worthy of the gospel (Philippians 1:27) and to let our lights shine before others so that they may see our good works and give glory to God (Matthew 5:16). We are called to put off the old self and to put on the qualities of Christ as His representatives (Colossians 3:10). Each command implies a care for how we externally present ourselves to others. Avoiding these commands reveals our hearts being rooted in the desire to exalt and worship self. Obeying these commands reveals our hearts being rooted in the desires to honor and exalt Christ and not only appear to be doing so.

Idolizing our appearance leads us to believe there is a better way of presenting ourselves than as representatives of Christ. It is as if we throw off the royal robe of righteousness to re-clothe ourselves in filthy rags. There is no appearance more valuable than that of heirs with Jesus Christ. As we believe this truth down to our core, we find confidence and assurance solely in our blood-bought salvation that has brought us into the family of God. We have the opportunity as Christians to be living, breathing examples of the gospel with our appearance. Our lives can reflect the good news of Jesus to all who see and listen. May we flee from the temptation to exalt ourselves and lead a life that exalts Jesus Christ with our hearts and actions.

Scripture reminds us that we are representatives of Christ, called to reflect Him with our lives to a watching world.

QUESTIONS

WHAT IS THE IDOL OF APPEARANCE? HOW MIGHT YOU BE TEMPTED TO MAKE
AN IDOL OUT OF YOUR APPEARANCE?

IN WHAT WAYS CAN THE IDOL OF APPEARANCE TEMPT YOU TO SIN?

HOW DOES SCRIPTURE CALL US TO LIVE AS REPRESENTATIVES OF CHRIST?
HOW DOES THIS INVOLVE PUTTING OFF BEING REPRESENTATIVES OF OURSELVES?
(READ COLOSSIANS 3:1-17)

HOW CAN WE REPLACE THE IDOL OF APPEARANCE WITH A DESIRE TO
REPRESENT CHRIST WITH OUR LIVES?

WEEK 2
/
DAY 3

"

OUR BODIES ARE NOT
TO BE WORSHIPED
BUT TO BE
vessels for worship.

"

BODY IMAGE

Body Image

READ 1 CORINTHIANS 6:19-20, EPHESIANS 2:10,
PHILIPPIANS 3:20-21

There are many things that can cross our mind when we look at ourselves in a full-length mirror. Where do we turn to tell us what we see? If we look to those around us, body images taunt us at every turn. We can quickly become unsatisfied with our bodies as we are laying out by the pool, shopping for jeans, or even going to the gym. If we look to culture, we find magazine covers, social media images, and celebrities curated and groomed to present the ideal image. We are riddled with ideas of the perfect body image.

We may find it difficult not to compare ourselves or question our figure, so we consume ourselves with questions. Why am I so tall? Why are my hips so wide? Why is my waist not smaller? Why is my hair straight? Our thoughts about ourselves may be subtle or severe. Some of us may not be able to enjoy a meal without wondering how it will affect our waistline. Maybe we cannot go anywhere without obsessing over how we look, or we are unable to be around others without comparing our figures. Some of us may obsess over dieting or working out and maybe even restrict our eating to measure up to the ideal image in our minds. Others of us may find that we spend an excessive amount of money on products and cosmetic help to better our appearance. Idolizing our body image begins by looking to these things to satisfy our longing to perfect our reflection.

As we look into the mirror, our bodies tell the story of a creation, moaning and groaning to be perfected.

As a result of the fall, our bodies are broken images. We bear the aches, pains, scars, and flaws of a sin-infested world. We cannot hide stretch marks, jiggly arms, or acne. We cannot stop gray hairs, wrinkles, or aging spots. As we look into the mirror, our bodies tell the story of a creation, moaning and groaning to be perfected. There are many things the world will present with the promise of redeeming our broken image. But when we look to the wrong place to perfect our image or fix what is broken, we find ourselves in an ever-evolving, ever-changing, over-promising, and never-fulfilling pursuit.

There is only One who is capable of making all things new. When we put our faith and hope in Jesus Christ to save us from the brokenness of sin,

God promises to redeem our entire being from the inside out. Scripture refers to our bodies as earthly tents longing to put on their heavenly dwelling, and Jesus is our only hope for that realization. Our earthly tents were never created to be worshiped. Instead, God's Word tells us that our body is a temple, an intended dwelling place of the Spirit while we wait for heaven (1 Corinthians 6:19-20). This means that when we receive the Holy Spirit as a gift from God through salvation, our hearts, minds, and souls are being transformed to walk in the newness of life. Our bodies are not to be worshiped but to be vessels for worship. Purchased by the blood of Jesus on the cross, with the help of the Holy Spirit at work in us, our bodies are now able to do as God originally designed them to do and as they will do in heaven—worship Him in all things. Our greatest pursuit with indelible eternal value is not to glorify ourselves and our own image but to glorify God and His image.

Our bodies are wonderful and miraculous creations by God, intended to honor and worship Him. We are tempted towards idolatry when we look to the wrong things to tell us what we see. Scripture tells us what we should truly see—God's image bearers. Every bone structure, cell placement, genetic binding, and vital organ points us heavenward to the Creator who thought of every single detail needed to live and survive in earthly bodies. He is purposeful and intentional in every way he has crafted each of us together, and He makes no mistakes. Everything is intended to draw our hearts back to Him in worship. Scripture reminds us of true worth that is not found in a perfect body image but instead in bearing the image of God. Our hope in Christ for our bodies is not to obtain a better version of ourselves, to be more lovely, or to be more physically perfected in the eyes of the world. Our hope in Christ is to be made more and more into the likeness of Jesus so that we can grow to love Him, know Him, honor Him, and glorify Him more.

Scripture reminds us of true worth that is not found in a perfect body image, but instead found in bearing the image of God.

HOW MIGHT YOU BE TEMPTED TO IDOLIZE YOUR BODY IMAGE?

IN WHAT WAYS CAN OUR BODILY FLAWS LEAD US TO LONG FOR REDEMPTION?

HOW CAN WE USE OUR BODIES AS VESSELS OF WORSHIP?

WHAT HOPE DO WE HAVE FOR OUR BODIES?

"

WE ARE TO INVEST IN

eternal matters

INSTEAD OF INVESTING IN
THOSE THINGS WHICH
PROLONG THE TEMPORAL.

"

HEALTH AND MEDICINE

Health and Medicine

READ JOB 14:5, 1 TIMOTHY 4:6-10,
2 CORINTHIANS 4:16-18

Health and medicine are important concerns for many Christians. We want to live long and happy lives, and undoubtedly, that comes with caring about our health and wellness. There are many things that have vowed to give us a better and longer life. Exercise, sleep, healthy eating habits, low stress levels, and vitamin D are just a few things that promise to contribute to that end. Beyond that, there are many impressive new approaches and technological advancements in modern medicine to contribute as well. Chemotherapy fights cancerous cells. Vaccines can deter deadly viruses and diseases. Transplants literally allow us to replace vital organs that are failing. With access to so many resources, products, and advancements, we may grow dependent on them for lowering our health risks and prolonging our lives. We can be tempted to place our hope in health and medicine to satisfy our longing for a full and satisfying life.

Idolizing health and medicine can take many shapes and forms. There are numerous physical, mental, and emotional investments we can place hope in to give us the answers and grant us peace of mind. We may depend heavily on medication to relieve pain or heal us. We may depend on daily workout routines and eating habits. We may even depend on counseling and therapy sessions to improve our mental and physical conditions. These things can be helpful, but the more we become dependent on these things, the more we construct our lives around them and the more damage caused when those things are stripped away from us.

We can be tempted to place our hope in health and medicine to satisfy our longing for a full and satisfying life.

Though desiring to live a long and full life is natural for many of us, Scripture reminds us that our days are numbered and determined by God (Job 14:5). There is no amount of good health or medicine that will change what God has already planned for our lives. This is not to dishearten us but to remind us that earth is not our true and permanent home. It helps us to look at our lives realistically — spending our days purposefully and intentionally, knowing that we are not promised tomorrow. We are to invest in eternal matters instead of investing in those things which prolong the temporal.

Does this mean we neglect caring for our bodies and avoid the doctor's office? It certainly does not. We are biblically instructed to steward our bodies well in service to kingdom purposes. It is wise and important to show concern for our bodies and maintain a healthy lifestyle to the best of our abilities. God has created many brilliant, creative, and innovative people to bless the world with new ideas, new products, and new resources in the world of health and medicine. We can receive them as a gracious gift from the Lord. Yet, they only provide for us momentarily. Investing in spiritual matters will far outlast investing in our temporal bodies.

The ultimate hope for a life that lasts is found in Jesus Christ alone. Every temptation to idolize the things of this world is met with that simple and profound answer. We are aimless if we search to find hope in anything else. Though outwardly our bodies will age and fail overtime, Jesus is inwardly transforming us into His likeness every single day. He is preparing us for our eternal bodies that will never be touched with sickness, disease, or even death. Health and medicine will only provide temporarily, but Jesus offers us eternity. He is the only one who is able to fulfill the promise of a life that lasts.

Health and medicine will only provide temporarily, but Jesus offers us eternity.

IN WHAT WAYS ARE YOU TEMPTED TO IDOLIZE HEALTH AND MEDICINE?

HOW CAN WE STEWARD OUR LIVES WELL WITH THE UNDERSTANDING
THAT THIS LIFE IS TEMPORAL?

SALVATION IN JESUS CHRIST IS OUR ULTIMATE HOPE FOR A LIFE THAT LASTS.
HOW DOES THIS TRUTH EQUIP YOU TO BATTLE THE TEMPTATION TO IDOLIZE
HEALTH AND MEDICINE?

WEEK 2
/
DAY 5

"

WE NEED

greater nourishment

THAN FOOD COULD
EVER PROVIDE FOR US.

"

FOOD

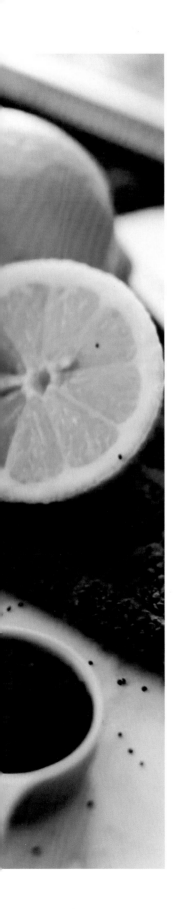

Food

READ PHILIPPIANS 3:19, 1 CORINTHIANS 6:12, JOHN 6:32-35

We have all likely seen the classic scene in romantic comedies when a woman experiences a break up and then proceeds to sit in front of a television with ice cream and chocolates to indulge in and comfort her flowing tears and aching heart. We see it often because it is relatable. Many of us have found ourselves in a place where it seemed the only thing that could console us was our favorite food. Idolization of food may seem far-fetched initially, but our hearts reveal misplaced worship when we run to it for more than sheer nutrition and sustenance. We may be tempted to run to food for comfort, consolation, pleasure, or relief. Food can be used as an escape or a glutinous indulgence.

When we look at the root of idolizing food, we are likely looking for a release from present circumstances. This may look like treating yourself to a pint of ice cream at the end of a stressful day. This may look like screaming at your child after they have interrupted you eating a meal in peace and quiet. It may even swing in the other direction of being ruled by food in such a way that leads you to obsessively count calories, yo-yo diet, or avoid it altogether. When food becomes more than it is intended to be, it begins to compete for the throne of your heart. This is why Paul says, "Food is for the stomach and the stomach for food" (1 Corinthians 6:13). He exhorts us that food is not to be consumed for any reason other than to feed our stomachs. It is not intended to support us emotionally, mentally, or spiritually.

When we look at the root of idolizing food, we are likely looking for a release from present circumstances.

God provides food for physical nourishment, but He has always made it clear that food is not enough for us. In the Bible, we see the example of the Israelites in the wilderness where life was hard, and people began to complain that it would be better to be back in slavery in Egypt, a place they had a plentiful amount of food to eat. In response to their complaints, God promises to "rain bread from heaven" (Exodus 16:4). When the morning came, the people saw that God had provided for them. He did so by providing them with bread but reminding them of their ultimate need for Him. Physically, we need food, and spiritually, we need God. Food will provide for us temporarily, but God's provision lasts forever. Food cannot comfort us or care for us, but God can. We need greater nourishment than food could ever provide for us. We find what we need only in the Bread of Life.

Food is a gift given to us to enjoy and utilize. Food can be a center staple for great conversation and rich fellowship. We can serve and bless others with food. There is great nutritional provision provided to us in food. God created food for good, and He created us to need food for nourishment. However, like every created thing, the delight we find in food is intended to point us back to our Creator. It is meant to lead us to worship Him for His continued provision and care. It is meant to point us in awe and delight of God who promises to satisfy us forever. We trash the food idol by eating and drinking to the glory of God. Every joyful experience found in food must end in heartfelt gratitude and praise to God. He is the true provider! Food must not ever get the glory, for there is only One to which it belongs.

Every joyful experience found in food must end in heartfelt gratitude and praise to God.

HOW ARE YOU TEMPTED TO MAKE AN IDOL OUT OF FOOD?

MAKE A LIST COMPARING AND CONTRASTING A GODLY VIEW OF FOOD
AND AN IDOLATROUS VIEW OF FOOD.

HOW CAN OUR APPETITE FOR FOOD BE USED TO CULTIVATE A
GREATER APPETITE FOR GOD?

My eager EXPECTATION AND HOPE is that I will not be ashamed about anything, but that now as always, with all courage, CHRIST WILL BE HIGHLY HONORED in my body, whether by life or by death.

Philippians 1:20

WEEK 2 SCRIPTURE MEMORY

Week Two Reflection

review all passages from this week

Paraphrase the passages that stood out to you the most this week.

_____
_____
_____
_____
_____
_____
_____
_____
_____
_____

What did you observe from this week's text about God and His character?

_____
_____
_____
_____
_____
_____
_____
_____
_____

What do these passages teach about the condition of mankind and about yourself?

_____
_____
_____
_____
_____
_____
_____
_____
_____

How do these passages point to the gospel?

_____
_____
_____
_____
_____
_____

How should you respond to these passages? What is the personal application?

_____
_____
_____
_____
_____
_____

What specific action steps can you take this week to apply these passages?

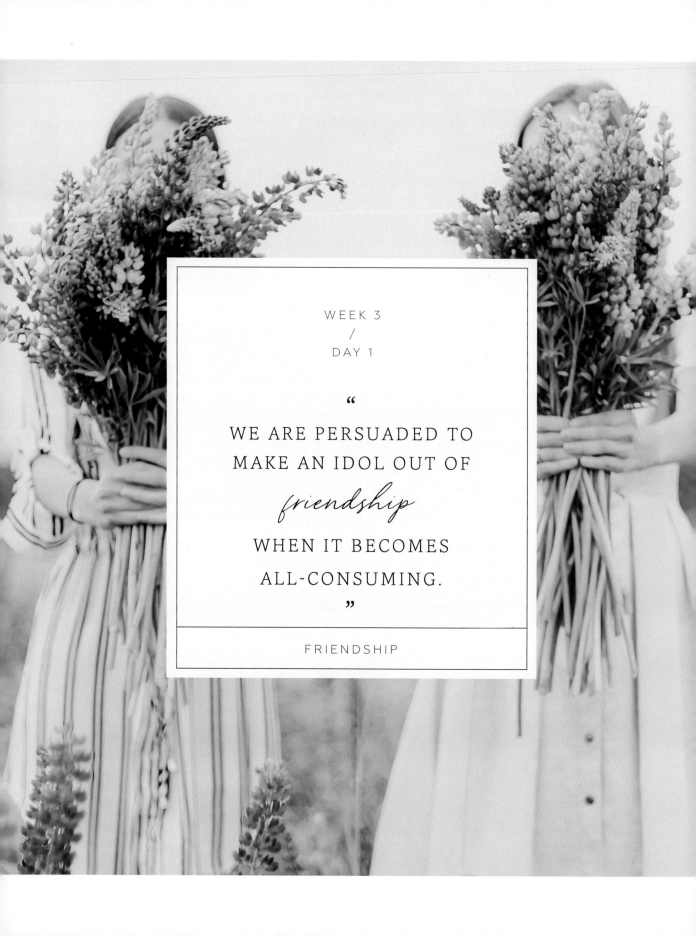

WEEK 3
/
DAY 1

"

WE ARE PERSUADED TO
MAKE AN IDOL OUT OF

friendship

WHEN IT BECOMES
ALL-CONSUMING.

"

FRIENDSHIP

Friendship

READ ECCLESIASTES 4:9-10, PROVERBS 17:17, JOHN 15:12-15

Friendship is such a wonderful gift. We are reminded through friendship that God gives us great joy in sharing our lives and experience with others. In a friend, we find companionship. We find a listening ear, a good laugh, shared interests, and the feeling of being known and understood by someone. Not only does friendship serve us well in the triumphs but also through the trials. We find a shoulder to cry on, a discerning word, and someone to share in our burdens. There are many ways we delight in finding a friend. God reiterates the benefit of relationships by declaring, "It is not good for the man to be alone" (Genesis 2:18). Relationships are profoundly orchestrated by God to be a good thing for His people. Yet, relational idolatry looms when we are tempted to make friendship or any other relationship a god for us.

We are reminded through friendship that God gives us great joy in sharing our lives and experience with others.

We are persuaded to make an idol out of friendship when it becomes all-consuming. Do I need a friend's validation to feel good about myself? Do I feel jealous or possessive when friends spend time together without me? Do I take more from friendship than I give? Do I place unrealistic expectations on my friends? Do I obsess over the possibility of losing a friendship? Is my identity rooted in this friendship? Do I find an unhealthy amount of security in this friendship? These questions are not exhaustive, but they can give us an idea of how relational idolatry can materialize in a friendship. These are important things when considering whether we have subtly misplaced our worship and redirected it toward friendship. If so, we have placed too much weight on a human being—a weight that only Jesus Christ can fully bear.

In Jeremiah 2:13, God speaks of His people forsaking Him for worthless idols. He says, "For my people have committed a double evil: they have abandoned me, the fountain of living water, and dug cisterns for themselves—cracked cisterns that cannot hold water." The image portrayed here is that His people are presented with an overflowing, unending, fresh fountain of water, yet they choose to go dig up canals to catch filthy, unfiltered, water in a vessel filled with cracks that would eventually go dry. This passage paints a visual representation of the hopelessness and foolishness found in idolizing something other than God. It is like digging up a broken cistern in search of nourishment when an ever-flowing river is right before our eyes.

Earthly friendship is a wonderful, beautiful, and vulnerable thing. But it does not belong on a throne. When we place our friendships on a pedestal, believing that one person can hold the weight of our misplaced demands, we set up good and godly friends to disappoint us constantly. Our friendships will become like a cistern, filled with cracks and holes as we expect it to hold an endless supply of nourishment for us. Relationships are crushed and bruised by such expectations. They end up broken and depleted by their efforts. A mere human was never created to bear such weight and expectation from another human. Instead, we were created to find those things in Christ and to live out the overflow of that profound hope.

When we feel secure in our relationship with Jesus, we will neither manipulate or use our friendships to feel secure, nor will we place unrealistic expectations on our friendships to make us feel worthy and valuable. When we find fulfillment in Jesus, we can give and serve in our friendship without needing to consume and take. When Jesus is seated on the throne of our hearts, we are freed up to enjoy friendship without being completely dependent on it. Our longing for true and full fellowship should never fall away from the hope of Jesus. People will fail us, but He is our perfect friend. Living in light of this truth opens the door for true, grace-filled, gospel-saturated friendship.

> When we feel secure in our relationship with Jesus, we will neither manipulate or use our friendships to feel secure, nor will we place unrealistic expectations on our friendships to make us feel worthy and valuable.

IN WHAT WAYS ARE YOU TEMPTED TO IDOLIZE FRIENDSHIP?

HOW HAVE YOU USED FRIENDSHIP AS A BROKEN CISTERN, EXPECTING IT
TO HOLD THE WEIGHT OF YOUR NEEDS? HOW MIGHT YOU PLACE EXPECTATIONS
ON FRIENDSHIP THAT ONLY JESUS CAN FULFILL?

HOW CAN WE SERVE OTHERS AND GLORIFY GOD IN OUR FRIENDSHIPS?

WEEK 3
/
DAY 2

"

WE BLUR THE IMAGE

of the gospel

WHEN WE USE MARRIAGE

AS A MEANS TO

MEET OUR NEEDS.

"

MARRIAGE

Marriage

READ EPHESIANS 5:22-33

Marriage, similar to friendship, is another relational gift God has provided for us to enjoy. Marriage, however, provides a much deeper and more devoted relationship with a spouse than any other relationship we will have on this side of heaven. There are profound joys in marriage—having someone to walk through the ups and downs of life with, someone to make decisions with, someone to share experiences with, someone to intimately enjoy, someone to love, and someone to cherish. Marriage goes beyond a friendship in that it is bound with a commitment and a promise. It is a relationship rooted in a covenant of love for one another.

Marriage was first instituted by God as a union of man and woman to be united under God in love, service, and commitment to one another. He established it, and it is good. But, His intentions for marriage go beyond sharing our lives with someone closely. Biblically, the purpose of marriage is to reflect the abounding love of Christ for His church. Marriage is intended to point us to our ultimate hope and longing for Christ to return and claim His bride, making marriage an exemplary picture of the gospel.

Biblically, the purpose of marriage is to reflect the abounding love of Christ for His church.

When we lose sight of the biblical purpose of marriage, we may be tempted to conjure up our own purpose for marriage. The first way is exhibited by those who are unmarried. From an early age, we may dream up our prince charming and our fairytale wedding. We imagine the qualities we may find in a husband and the story that will unfold when we meet. These thoughts evolve through the years, and we begin longing for a dating relationship to start the process of finding a spouse. The desire for companionship is natural and good. There is no fault in wanting marriage and searching for a spouse. However, as with anything, that pursuit becomes idolatrous when we are willing to do anything to get it. The desire for marriage becomes unhealthy when it rules our hearts and minds. If we believe it will satisfy the longings of our hearts for love and if every decision we make is centered around the pursuit of finding a spouse, it has become an idol. Idolatry has crept in when we cannot feel whole or complete without a spouse.

The second way is displayed by those who are in a committed marriage. If the marriage idol is not uprooted before the wedding day, it will only transform into idolizing our spouse in the same way. If our spouse is seated on the throne of our hearts, we will expect our spouse to display the attributes only God can possess. Attributes like loving us unconditionally, knowing us perfectly, listening and understanding our every thought and intention, knowing how to care for our deepest needs, never sinning against us, carrying our every burden, and fulfilling our every yearning—placing these types of expectations on our spouse not only sets our spouse up to hurt, fail, and disappoint us, but it can also be deeply wounding for that person. Your spouse was never created to be a god to us, nor could that ever be.

Though an incredible privilege and joy, marriage was never meant to meet our every need. Marriage is a temporary union intended to point us toward our eternal union with Christ. We blur the image of the gospel when we use marriage as a means to meet our needs. When two sinners are united together as one flesh, there will undoubtedly be short-comings, failures, and sins against one another. We display the gospel through constantly extending grace and walking in repentance. It reveals a greater need outside of our marriages—the hope and salvation of Jesus Christ. In Christ, we are perfectly understood in every thought, word, and deed. He cares for our deepest needs and comforts us in every way. He never sins against us. He carries every weight and burden we bear. He fulfills our every longing. He loves us unconditionally. When Christ is the recipient of our deepest affections and devotion, not only do we free ourselves up to enjoy and celebrate marriage in the way we are intended to, but we set our spouses free from our unattainable standards and expectations.

If our spouse is seated on the throne of our hearts, we will expect our spouse to display the attributes only God can possess.

HOW MIGHT YOU BE TEMPTED TO IDOLIZE MARRIAGE?

HOW DOES A BIBLICAL UNDERSTANDING OF MARRIAGE SHAPE YOUR
EXPECTATIONS FOR IT?

IN WHAT WAYS DOES THE IDOLATRY OF MARRIAGE HARM YOU AND YOUR
CURRENT OR FUTURE SPOUSE?

MARRIAGE CANNOT MEET OUR DEEPEST NEEDS, BUT CHRIST CAN. JOURNAL
THROUGH THE WAYS HE FULFILLS OUR GREATEST NEEDS.

WEEK 3
/
DAY 3

"

WE MUST PRAY FOR THIS
UNWAVERING BELIEF:
*He is more than
enough for us and
our children.*

"

CHILDREN

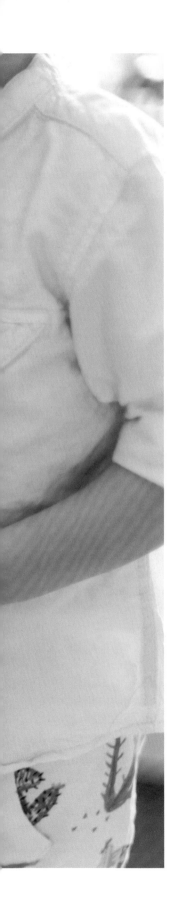

Children

READ GENESIS 22:15-18, MATTHEW 10:37-39,
PSALM 127:3-5

We have talked through a couple of types of relational idolatry. There are many specific relationships that we can struggle to idolize. The last type of relationship we are going to address in this study is making an idol of our children. Children are a blessing and a gift from the Lord. They further the lineage of humanity and bring a bright new perspective to the world. God fulfilled the promise of bringing His Son, Jesus Christ, to the world through generations and generations of children. We can celebrate and enjoy the wonderful gift of children in our lives. They add such joy, creativity, and adventure to our lives. Yet, like any good thing, we can be tempted to idolize our children. This may be one of the most commonly overlooked idols in that it can be mistaken for a deep love and nurturing care. We might easily convince ourselves that our relationship with our children is not idolatrous. However, we must look clearly at our heart and motives to relate and love in a way that honors God and serves our children.

God fulfilled the promise of bringing His Son, Jesus Christ, to the world through generations and generations of children.

This idol can take shape in a number of ways as children grow and age. When we first desire to have children, it can become an all-consuming thought and pursuit. The absence of conception may leave us feeling hopeless and disappointed as we wait. Every passing month with no positive line can leave us wanting children more than anything else. In the case that we cannot have children, we may feel empty, hopeless, and without purpose. This brings our idolatry to the forefront. When the hope for children rules our hearts and minds, we have put that desire on the throne of our hearts. We hope in it to fill the void and longing, and we find ourselves discontent without it.

Once we bring children into the world, the idol just takes on different forms and changes through the years. It might look like living our lives to be fulfilled through our children. It might mean using our children to feel successful, approved, or valuable. It could mean placing our identity in our children or in our ability to parent them. It could mean constantly comparing our children to others and placing unrealistic expectations on them. It might look like being consumed by caring for them perfectly. It may even mean doing anything to feel needed and depended on by them.

The story of Abraham and Isaac provides an interesting and important example for how we should view our children. In Genesis 22, God commands Abraham to take his son, Isaac, to the land of Moriah, up on a mountain to offer him as a sacrifice. This was the son God promised to Abraham to bring about generations of offspring as numerous as the stars. Abraham could have easily questioned this command, become possessive over his son, and refused. But Abraham's trust in the Lord was evident. When the two arrived at the mountain, Isaac saw the fire and the wood and questioned, "but where is the lamb for the burnt offering?" Abraham replied, "God himself will provide the lamb for the offering, my son" (Genesis 22:7-8). Abraham was entrusting his son to the Lord, even though he was uncertain of what was going to take place. God tested Abraham. Abraham knew that he could trust God. He knew God cared for and loved Isaac even more than he did. He was confident in God's provision over his own, even if he did not understand it. And at the last moment, God provided the sacrifice. Abraham's son was spared.

We are reminded through the example of Abraham and Isaac that our children belong ultimately to the Lord. This understanding can be sobering and difficult to understand at times. Our children are not our own but have been entrusted to us for a time to love, care for, and to train them up in godliness. In doing so, we are provided numerous opportunities to hand our children to the Lord and trust in Him. We regularly face mishaps, sin, worldly influences, and trouble that could leave us tightly gripping our children in fear of what may happen if we are not watching his or her every movement. God provides every opportunity to take our children off the throne of our hearts and look fully and dependently to Him. Will we shrink at the thought, or will we willingly receive God's greater provision and care over our lives and our children's lives?

We turn from idolatry, regardless of where our misplaced worship is directed, ultimately by feeding ourselves with the truth of God's character, believing His Word, and entrusting our lives and worship to the divine Creator and Sustainer of the universe. When our hearts are in tune with the true nature of God, our efforts resemble grains of sand in contrast to a mighty mountain. We must pray for this unwavering belief: He is more than enough for us and our children. As we rightly place God on the throne of our hearts, we not only free ourselves up from the bondage of idolizing our children, but we free our children up from the pressure of living to fulfill our every expectation. Additionally, we model before them an ultimate hope and trust, not in any earthly relationship but in our good Father in heaven.

Our children are not our own but have been entrusted to us for a time
to love, care for, and to train them up in godliness.

IN WHAT WAYS ARE YOU TEMPTED TO IDOLIZE YOUR CHILDREN OR
YOUR DESIRE FOR CHILDREN?

HOW ARE YOU AFFECTED BY THE STORY OF ABRAHAM AND ISAAC? IN WHAT WAYS
MIGHT YOU BE TEMPTED TO DISTRUST GOD WITH YOUR CHILDREN?

HOW CAN YOU LOVE AND CARE FOR YOUR CHILDREN WITH ULTIMATE DEPENDENCE
ON THE LORD? HOW CAN YOU CULTIVATE A DEEPER TRUST IN HIM?

WEEK 3
/
DAY 4

"

WHEN A TRADITION IS
ELEVATED TO THE PLACE
OF A LAW OR BIBLICAL
PRACTICE, THAT TRADITION
has become an idol.

"

TRADITIONS

Traditions

READ MARK 7:1-13

There is something about traditions that make us feel connected to those who have walked before us. Holiday traditions abound with feasts and family practices curated in their own ways and carried down through the years. Heirlooms are passed down and treasured through generations. Customs are upheld by churches who have followed those before them. We see tradition all around us. Traditions are customs, beliefs, and practices that are passed down from generation to generation. They can serve as a means of uniting the past and the present. They give us tangible practices, created and enacted for a certain purpose by those who felt it important. We can enjoy and celebrate those good and helpful traditions as we continue to implement them in our present era and utilize the knowledge of a previous time.

As we think about traditions, there are many things to consider. Traditions for Christians must always be developed and continued under the banner of glorifying God in everything we do. Anything we do must flow from the command, "whether you eat or drink, or whatever you do, do everything for the glory of God" (1 Corinthians 10:31). This is an important principle for considering traditions. Some traditions we continue in today without any real knowledge of why we do them. As years pass and generations follow, the origin and purpose of the traditions can often get lost along the way. We have no real understanding of whether the origin stemmed from good or harmful intentions. Yet, we continue on for the sake of upholding the tradition. Additionally, there are traditions we later realize to be hurtful, insensitive, or dishonoring to the Lord. They may prove to be exclusive toward outsiders. They may cause division and arguments. They may even lead to sinful thoughts or actions. We must ask ourselves if this tradition honors the Lord and serves others. If it does not do that, we must be willing to let go of anything standing in the way of our full allegiance to Jesus.

Traditions for Christians must always be developed and continued under the banner of glorifying God in everything we do.

Traditions can become idolatrous when we hold them to a higher standard than honoring the Lord. If we are unable to let go of or relinquish a tradition that is clearly dishonoring the Lord or that is an unloving disservice to others, it has become an idol. When a tradition is elevated to the place of a law or biblical practice, that tradition has become an idol. Mark 7 sheds light on idolizing traditions. Pharisees came from Jerusalem to see Jesus and His disciples. They immediately began questioning why they did not uphold a tradition of the elders. The specific tradition they referred to was an elaborate ceremonial hand washing that came before partaking of bread, a tradition the disciples had not upheld. Jesus' response to the Pharisees exposed the reality of their hearts. As we have mentioned previously in this study, the Pharisees cared far more about their appearance of righteousness than about the actual pursuit of righteousness. Jesus rebuked their hypocrisy when he said, "You nullify the Word of God by your tradition that you have handed down. And you do many other similar things" (Mark 7:13). He confronted their hypocritical practice of elevating their traditions over the Word of God and implementing them to the equivalence of the law. It was evident that their traditions only honored themselves, demonstrating no regard for honoring and glorifying the Lord.

With everything, we must evaluate the motives of our hearts and ask ourselves the tough questions. Traditions can be a treasure when held in their proper place. What is the purpose of this tradition? How does this tradition honor the Lord and serve others? Why do I find this tradition important enough to continue? These are all important questions to ask as we plan and execute certain customs and practices in our communities, homes, and churches. May we pray and ask God to saturate our hearts and minds with the aim to glorify God in everything we do, and may we be equipped to fight against anything else that contends for our ultimate loyalty.

With everything, we must evaluate the motives of our hearts and ask ourselves the tough questions. Traditions can be a treasure when held in their proper place.

HOW HAVE YOU BEEN TEMPTED TO IDOLIZE TRADITIONS?

IN WHAT WAYS, LIKE THE PHARISEES, HAVE YOU ELEVATED A TRADITION TO THE PLACE OF LAW OR BIBLICAL NECESSITY?

HOW CAN WE ENJOY TRADITIONS IN A WAY THAT IS HONORING TO THE LORD AND THAT IS IN SERVICE OF OTHERS?

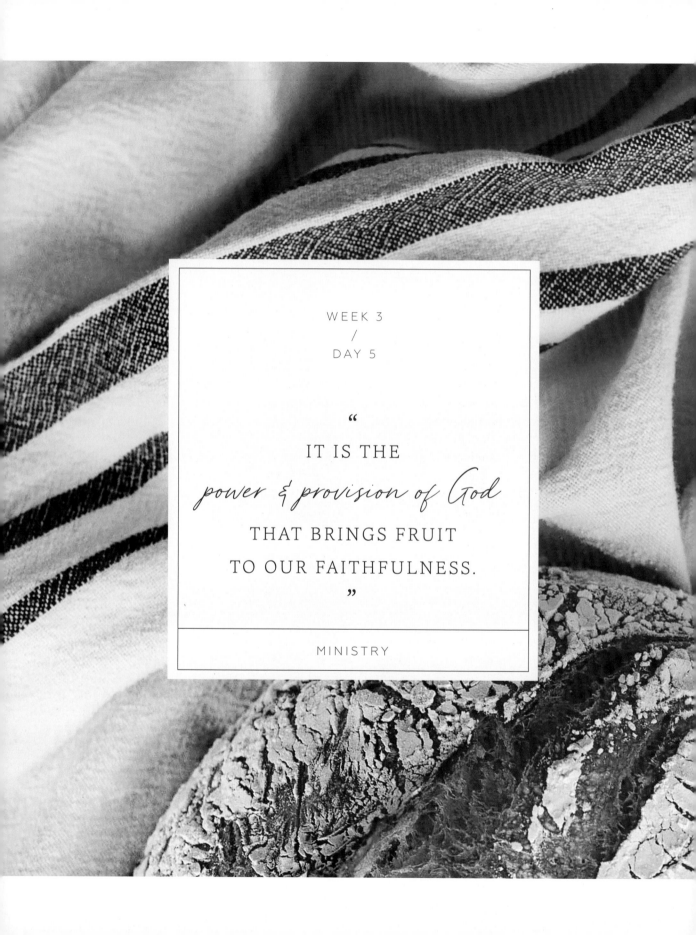

WEEK 3
/
DAY 5

"

IT IS THE

power & provision of God

THAT BRINGS FRUIT

TO OUR FAITHFULNESS.

"

MINISTRY

Ministry

READ 2 CORINTHIANS 5:18-21, HEBREWS 13:20-21,
1 CORINTHIANS 3:5-7

Ministry is a necessary part of the Christian life. Everyone who follows Jesus follows His steps in the ministry of sharing the good news of the gospel. Just as we are brought into the family of God through salvation, so we are brought into the ministry of Jesus. The Great Commission serves as a command for all Christians to, "Go, therefore, and make disciples of all nations, baptizing them in the name of the Father and of the Son and of the Holy Spirit, teaching them to observe everything I have commanded you..." (Matthew 28:19-20). Ministry, however, does not look the same for every Christian. For some of us, it is vocational, and for others it is not. For some of us, we are surrounded by ample opportunities for ministry, and for others we are not. Though ministry does not look the same for every Christian, every Christian is called to ministry. Our unique personalities, giftings, and experiences, specifically given to us by God, allow us to minister the truth of the gospel in different ways through various settings and circumstances. This is the beauty of the body of Christ. We each contribute to the ministry of the gospel in a special and necessary way.

Though ministry does not look the same for every Christian,
every Christian is called to ministry.

The ultimate aim of Christian ministry is to make Jesus known. Every way we are equipped to join in this ministry is given and established by God. We cannot do it on our own. It is God alone who opens blind eyes and softens hard hearts. We are merely vessels for His intended purposes. It is the power and provision of God that brings fruit to our faithfulness. This should always remain at the forefront of all our ministry efforts. When the purpose of our ministry becomes something else, we may be tempted to idolize it. If we search for identity, success, or recognition in ministry, it has become an idol. If ministry is about serving others to get something in return, it has become an idol. If ministry becomes a performance for others to see, it has become an idol. If we claim to be leading people to follow Jesus but are really leading them to follow us, beware of idolatry. Idolizing ministry can be dangerous in that outwardly it looks honorable whilst inwardly it is dishonoring to the

Lord. We can easily continue in our ways with seemingly few external consequences. But the motives of the heart are not hidden from God.

The heart of this idol is using and abusing a God-glorifying task to glorify ourselves. Not only is idolizing ministry a disservice to others, it is a disservice to ourselves. By entertaining how we can be praised, admired, or rewarded for our ministry efforts, we are unloving toward those we claim to serve, and we place sinful stumbling blocks in front of ourselves. When we place too much emphasis on ministry to fulfill us, we waver with the seasons. We may grow prideful when successful, even placing dependency on others to fuel our pride and need for recognition. We may fall victim to spiritual greed, using our ministry to climb the ladder of fame and fortune. When our ministry is lacking in fruit or we feel little recognition, we may feel lost or purposeless. We may even become stagnant and unwilling in our efforts. Ultimately idolizing ministry leads us to find our deepest joy and delight in the act of serving Jesus, rather than in Jesus himself.

When we identify the idol of ministry in our lives, we must actively fight against it. We fight the dangers of placing it on the throne of our hearts by not only preaching the gospel to others but by preaching the gospel to ourselves. Our ministry efforts should always be out of an overflow of the grace of God we received when we came to know Jesus as our Lord and Savior. Our ministry should always be a reflection of Jesus. Additionally, we must surround ourselves with those who can continually hold us accountable for our motives in ministry. We need other Christians around us to point out sinful patterns, hard truths, and challenge us in our approaches. Accountability provides a safety net for any temptation to misdirect our worship in ministry. Ministry is a privilege appointed to those who believe that Jesus is the answer to our deepest needs and longings. May our ministry efforts always and only reflect that hope.

Our ministry should always be a reflection of Jesus.

IN WHAT WAYS MIGHT YOU BE TEMPTED TO IDOLIZE MINISTRY?

IN WHAT WAYS CAN MINISTRY BE ABUSED TO GLORIFY
SELF INSTEAD OF GLORIFY GOD?

HOW CAN WE FIGHT THE TEMPTATION TO IDOLIZE MINISTRY?

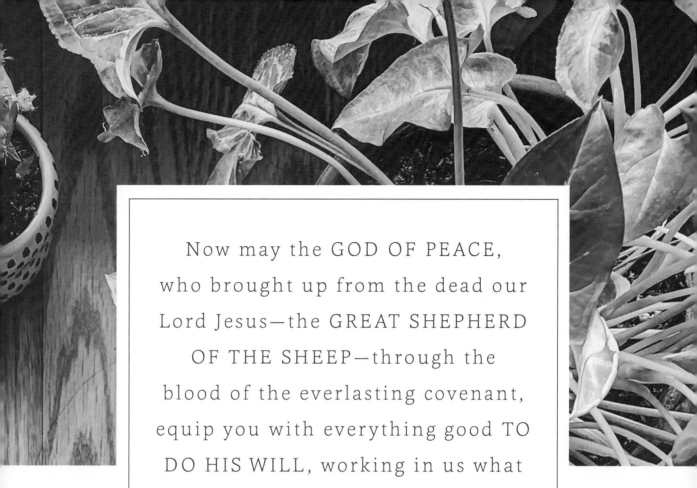

Now may the GOD OF PEACE, who brought up from the dead our Lord Jesus—the GREAT SHEPHERD OF THE SHEEP—through the blood of the everlasting covenant, equip you with everything good TO DO HIS WILL, working in us what is pleasing in his sight, through Jesus Christ, to whom be GLORY FOREVER AND EVER. Amen.

Hebrews 13:20–21

WEEK 3 SCRIPTURE MEMORY

Week Three Reflection

review all passages from this week

Paraphrase the passages that stood out to you the most this week.

_____
_____
_____
_____
_____
_____
_____
_____
_____
_____

What did you observe from this week's text about God and His character?

_____
_____
_____
_____
_____
_____
_____
_____
_____

What do these passages teach about the condition of mankind and about yourself?

_____
_____
_____
_____
_____
_____
_____
_____
_____

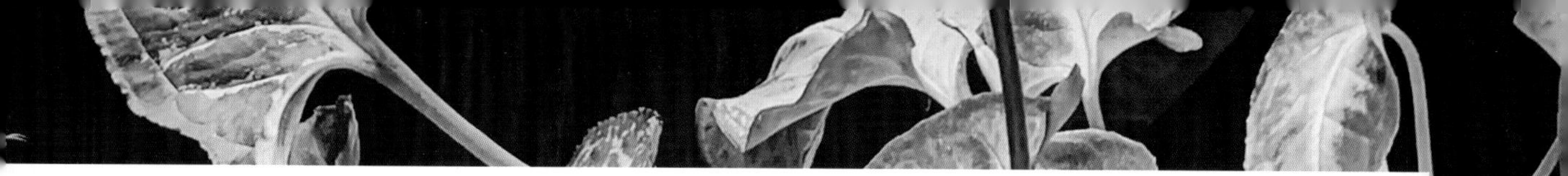

How do these passages point to the gospel?

_____

_____

_____

_____

_____

_____

How should you respond to these passages? What is the personal application?

_____

_____

_____

_____

_____

_____

What specific action steps can you take this week to apply these passages?

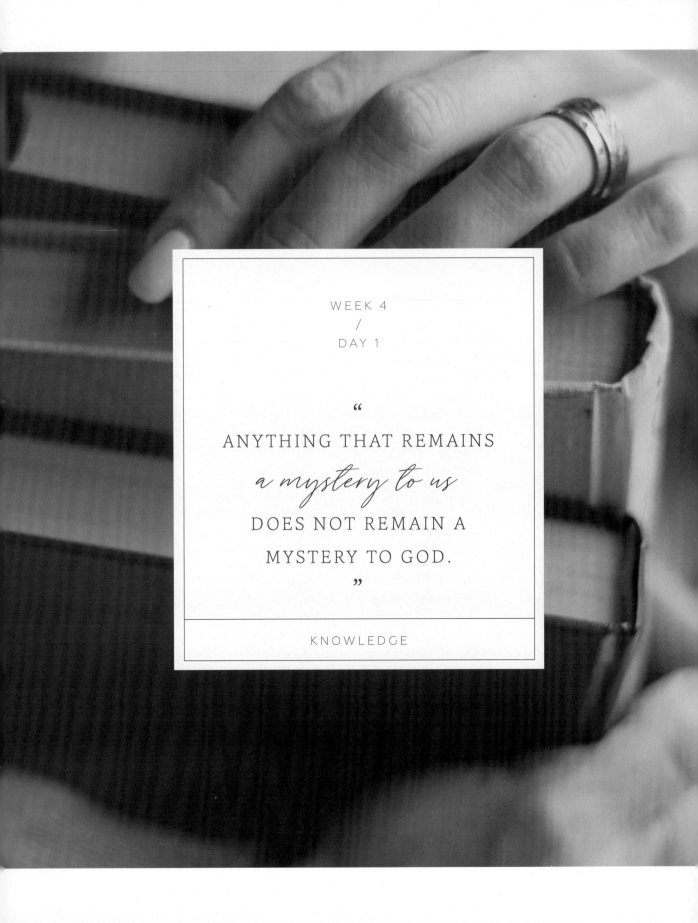

WEEK 4
/
DAY 1

"

ANYTHING THAT REMAINS

a mystery to us

DOES NOT REMAIN A

MYSTERY TO GOD.

"

KNOWLEDGE

Knowledge

READ ROMANS 1:21-22, 1 CORINTHIANS 3:18-20, DEUTERONOMY 29:29

The pursuit of knowledge begins at an early age as we spend the bulk of our days in some form of educational setting. From elementary school to college, we are surrounded with opportunities to gain knowledge that will carry with us throughout life and work. We are taught formulas, theories, standards, and definitions to prepare us to function and develop in society. All that is provided to help us know and understand the way the world functions is a gift from God. For Christians, there is a greater source of knowledge — the Bible. God has given us His Word so that we can know and love Him better. We search the Scriptures to gain knowledge and understanding about who God is and how He calls us to live in this world. Knowing Him more cultivates our love for Him. Loving Him filters into the way we think, speak, act, and live. Every way that we can learn and grow, with God at the forefront, better equips and prepares us to navigate through this journey called life.

> *The Tree of Knowledge of Good and Evil is a symbol for our tendency to exalt our own knowledge over the loving knowledge of God.*

God reveals that He makes known to man what He wants to make known and that mysteries remain only for Him to know (Deuteronomy 29:29). We can be tempted to obtain knowledge in a way we were not created to. Even with the access we have been provided to know God and understand the world, we might seek it out in an idolatrous way. When Adam and Eve were tempted to eat of the forbidden fruit, the serpent lured them in with a promise to be like God, knowing good and evil. One of the reasons Eve ultimately partook of the fruit was because it was, "desirable for obtaining wisdom" (Genesis 3:6). They believed the lie that God was holding out on them, and they followed their idolatrous desire for knowledge. The Tree of Knowledge of Good and Evil is a symbol for our tendency to exalt our own knowledge over the loving knowledge of God. Adam and Eve sacrificed the latter for the former. How many of us are willing to do the same?

Exalting knowledge as an idol is reflected in our lives in different ways. It may look like being financially consumed by the pursuit of degrees. It might look like being consumed by the idea of knowing and comprehending more than others. It may produce a lack of humility and understanding when facing those differing viewpoints. It may leave us discontent in our intellectual findings, continually desiring more. It may even leave us searching for answers within ourselves, neglecting the endless source of wisdom found in God. But what is the end result? They become fools. True knowledge was never intended to be found in ourselves.

We are limited in every capacity. At some point, our accumulated knowledge comes to a halt. There are things our feeble minds cannot fathom, and there are things of this world we will not comprehend. And yet, God has created us with minds to know Him more deeply than any other form of creation. He is delighted in being known by us. He offers an eternal fountain of wisdom to us through His Word. It is inexhaustibly filled with the knowledge of who God is and how we are to live in light of that knowledge. He has provided us everything we need for life and godliness. Anything that remains a mystery to us does not remain a mystery to God. He is not like us. He is not limited in knowledge and understanding. He knows all, sees all, and understands all, beyond what we can even imagine. This should serve as a comfort to us. Even in our intellectual shortcomings, we are not left without answers. We are not left to create a god for ourselves. There is someone greater and more glorious for us to put our hope and faith in. God is the beginning and end of all wisdom. As we seek to know and understand more, we can filter all our findings through that resounding reality.

All that is provided to help us know and understand the way the world functions is a gift from God.

HOW MIGHT YOU BE TEMPTED TO IDOLIZE THE PURSUIT OF KNOWLEDGE?

IN WHAT WAYS DO YOU ELEVATE YOUR OWN KNOWLEDGE OVER THE KNOWLEDGE OF GOD?

WHAT DOES THE BIBLE HAVE TO SAY ABOUT THOSE WHO CLAIM TO BE WISE?

HOW CAN YOU CULTIVATE A GREATER KNOWLEDGE FOR GOD IN HIS WORD? HOW MIGHT THIS ULTIMATELY LEAD YOU TO TRUST HIM IN THE UNKNOWN THINGS OF THIS WORLD?

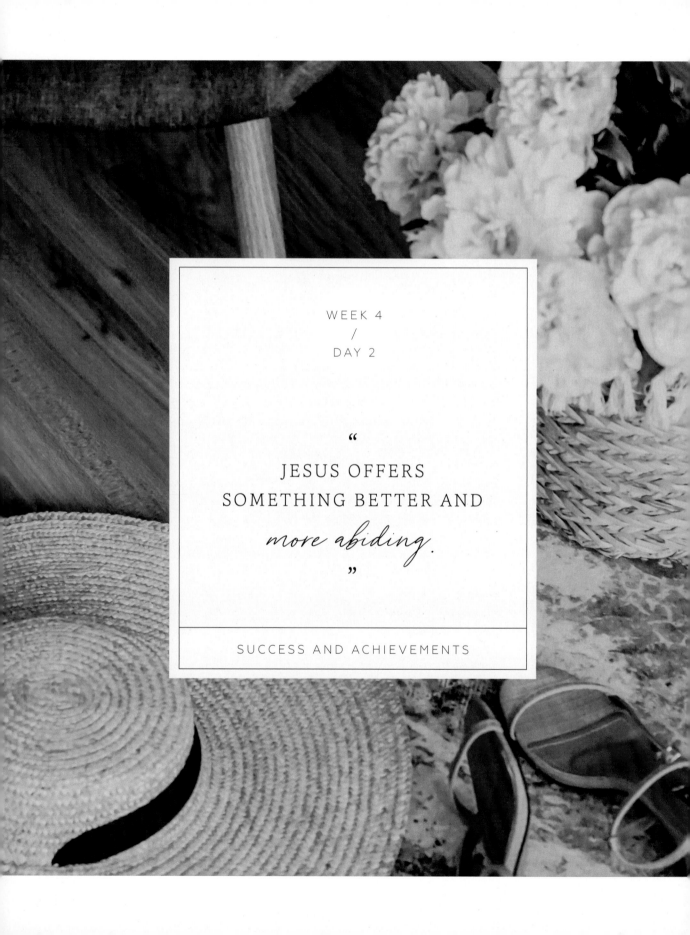

WEEK 4
/
DAY 2

"

JESUS OFFERS
SOMETHING BETTER AND
more abiding.

"

SUCCESS AND ACHIEVEMENTS

Success and Achievements

READ 1 CORINTHIANS 1:26-31, JOHN 3:27

Have you ever tried to imagine yourself standing on the top platform at the award ceremony of the Olympics, awaiting the placement of a bright and shiny gold medal around your neck? Can you imagine the honor? The feeling of accomplishment? The recognition of all your efforts? We can likely imagine that the emotion is astounding. Great success and achievement can leave us on cloud nine. From attendance awards to graduation diplomas to substantial job promotions, there is a substantial feeling of accomplishment when we have achieved something really special. Success can open the door for job opportunities, financial provision, recognition, and respect. When we work hard for something, it is affirming to be rewarded for it. It is easy to continue on in our efforts when we feel it has been properly observed and valued.

The desire to succeed and achieve can be intentional and purposeful when grounded in the understanding that everything we have been given comes from God. Our success can be a platform to display the grace and provision of God to those who have watched us succeed. We can use our accomplishments to serve and bless others. We can thrive in our field of interest in a way that uses our abilities and strengths to the glory of God. Temptation accompanies success when we want to claim our achievements as our own. Whether in our jobs, in our parenting, in sports, or in ministry, if our inclination is to boast in ourselves, we begin misdirecting our worship to ourselves and our efforts. We feed the lie that we have succeeded in our own strengths, without giving glory where it is due. Furthermore, we can become greedy for more. We can grow discontent in less favorable outcomes. We can be consumed by the need to feel worth through our advances. We may even become riddled with bitterness, blaming others for our shortcomings.

We can use our accomplishments to serve and bless others.

Referring back to that Olympic platform—astounding emotions, yes. But what happens in the next few months? Years? Decades? Even at the pinnacle of success, it is only short-lived. That feeling of prominence and notability subsides. Should the ultimate aim be to claim and attain success, the pursuit would be endless. We would never feel satisfied until we could stand on that top platform again, and even then, it would only satisfy us temporarily. We would become like hamsters in a wheel, trapped in a never-ending cycle, chasing success to the point of exhaustion. It will leave us emptier and emptier with every attempt.

Jesus offers something better and more abiding. We can squash the need to feel as if we have done something great, because Jesus has already done it. He has done what no man could ever do. He conquered sin and defeated the grave. He made the ultimate sacrifice to offer us eternal life in Him so that we could conquer it too. There is truly nothing with more profound value and worth for this life and all eternity than life in Christ. We may not stand at the top of an Olympic platform in this lifetime, but because of salvation in Christ, we can stand in victory forever. This is the kind of victory we anticipate—the kind of victory that makes gold medals, notoriety, and affluence look like rubbish. It is truly the greatest accomplishment that we could ever associate to our name—to know and enjoy God forever. May every success in this lifetime leave us in awe and worship of God who has brought all things to be.

We may not stand at the top of an Olympic platform in this lifetime, but because of salvation in Christ, we can stand in victory forever.

IN WHAT WAYS MIGHT YOU BE TEMPTED TO IDOLIZE YOUR SUCCESS
AND ACHIEVEMENTS?

HOW CAN YOU USE SUCCESS TO GLORIFY GOD AND SERVE OTHERS?

THE GREATEST VICTORY WE COULD EVER BE OFFERED IS IN JESUS CHRIST.
HOW DOES THIS TRANSFORM THE WAY WE VIEW SUCCESS AND ACHIEVEMENT?

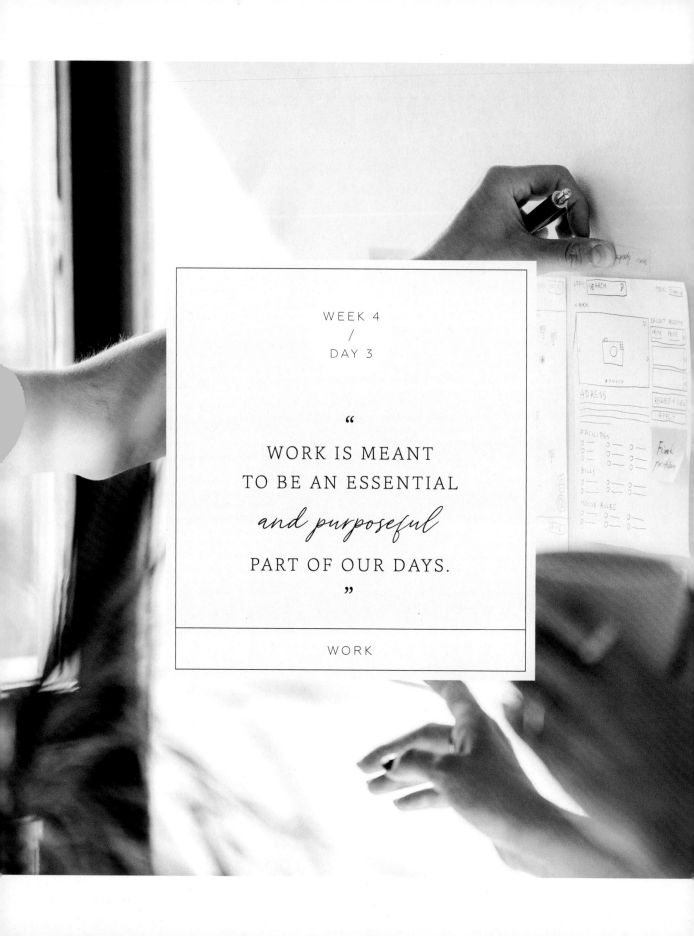

WEEK 4
/
DAY 3

"

WORK IS MEANT
TO BE AN ESSENTIAL
and purposeful
PART OF OUR DAYS.

"

WORK

Work

READ GENESIS 2:15, EPHESIANS 2:8–10,
1 CORINTHIANS 15:58

We were created to work. We see this intention in Genesis 2:15: "The Lord God took the man and placed him in the garden of Eden to work it and watch over it." This was a role given to Adam and Eve in the garden of Eden and was part of God's design before sin entered into the world. He is the author of work. Work is meant to be an essential and purposeful part of our days. Whether working a paid position or working in the home to care for family, our days are filled with active work to be returned to God in glory.

God has given us the privilege to enjoy and appreciate our work. He has created us to be inspired, ambitious, and motivated with many gifts and talents to contribute to the world. He has given us unique roles and opportunities specific to His plans and purposes for our work. Work is a good thing. However, seeking fulfillment in a job, career, or any other sort of work, leads us to elevate it to a position where it does not belong. We were created to worship God with our work, not worship our work. You may be able to identify this temptation if you find yourself struggling with the following things: Do you place more value on your time at work than your time with God? Do you constantly think about your job, the tasks that need to be completed, and the projects that loom? Do you constantly check your emails? Does work constantly leave you anxious and stressed? Do you work to the point of exhaustion every day? Are you persistently looking for work that will satisfy your every need? Is it the first thing you think of when you wake up in the morning? These are questions we can ask ourselves to help identify the idol of work in our lives.

We were created to worship God with our work, not worship our work.

Our work is meant to be useful and fruitful but never to be placed on a pedestal. We must remain on guard toward the tendency to allow work to pull at our heart's affections. We can fight against the temptation to idolize work by designating a certain portion of our day to work and upholding those boundaries. We can evaluate the sacrifices we make to uphold our work obligations and consider whether they honor the Lord and serve our family. We can start or end our days reading the Bible to saturate our hearts and minds with the truth of Scripture instead of emails and tasks to be done. We can invite others into our work, frequently asking them if it has become too consuming. We must preach the gospel to ourselves which frees us to work wholeheartedly as unto the Lord. The gospel liberates us from the pressure to prove and fulfill ourselves through what we do and opens the door to pursue the true purpose of work as a vessel of worship.

Although we live in a world corrupted by sin, God has promised redemption. He is actively redeeming all things, including work. If all things were to disappear and go to waste, why would there be a need to care about work at all? Our jobs would simply be forms of survival for the here and now. But because God intentionally instructs us to work, we can be certain there is greater purpose in what we do beyond this lifetime. In the new heavens and new earth, our work will continue, and our gifts, talents, abilities, and skills will be used to bless others and worship God! It will be brought to full expectation of what God originally intended for it to be. Therefore, our aim should be to work with eternal intent instead of being consumed with worldly or self-exalting standards of work. We are to use every opportunity in our labor and toil to glorify God.

Our work is meant to be useful and fruitful but never to be placed on a pedestal. We must remain on guard toward the tendency to allow work to pull at our heart's affections.

HOW HAVE YOU BEEN TEMPTED TO IDOLIZE WORK?

IN WHAT WAYS ARE WE CREATED TO WORSHIP GOD WITH OUR WORK?
HOW CAN WE USE IT TO GLORIFY GOD AND BLESS OTHERS?

IN WHAT WAYS CAN WE FIGHT THE TEMPTATION TO IDOLIZE OUR WORK?

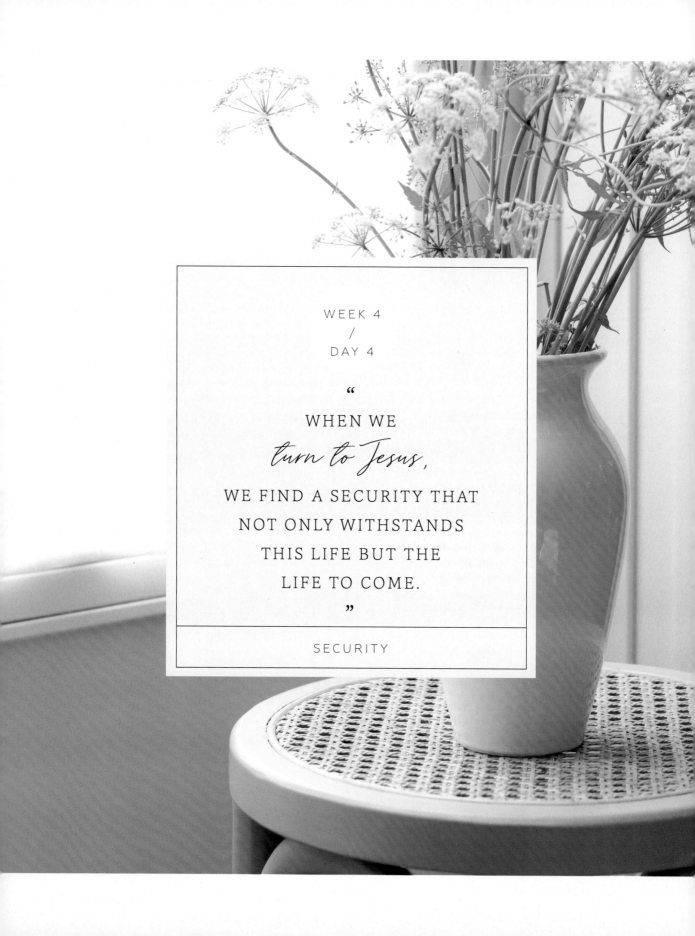

WEEK 4
/
DAY 4

"

WHEN WE
turn to Jesus,
WE FIND A SECURITY THAT
NOT ONLY WITHSTANDS
THIS LIFE BUT THE
LIFE TO COME.

"

SECURITY

Security

READ MATTHEW 14:28-31, 1 THESSALONIANS 5:1-3

Regardless of who we are, where we come from, or what stage of life we are in, we all long to feel secure. Whether in our careers, financial plans, relationships, health, or in things as simple as an alarm system, we all look for ways to feel safer and certain of our situations. Security appears to provide us protection from the unnerving unknown surrounding us. We often associate security with stability in that we long to feel that we have addressed every possible area of concern in our lives. There is nothing wrong about making sure you have enough money to pay the bills, making sure you have a roof over your head, or regularly visiting the doctor to check on your health. However, these good things become a threat when we turn them into ultimate things. When things of this world threaten our security, how do we respond? Do you run with full abandon to the God you trust in wholeheartedly to provide and care for you? Or do you turn to self-preservation, doing everything you can to secure the things that are under attack?

When things of this world threaten our security how do we respond?

True security cannot be found within ourselves or even in the ways we may be tempted to find it. The story of Peter in Matthew 14 serves as one of many examples for our efforts to feel secure in the wind and waves of life. Jesus is seen by His disciples walking on the water, and they are terrified. Jesus immediately relieves their fears by speaking to them saying, "Have courage! It is I. Don't be afraid" (Matthew 14:27). He calms their fears by pointing them to Himself. Peter proceeds by following Jesus' command to come and walk to Him on the water. As soon as Peter takes his eyes off of Jesus, he sees the strength of the wind and waves and begins to sink, crying out for help. Though Peter externally responded with courage, Jesus takes hold of him and unveils his internal lack of faith. Though Peter seemed to trust fully in Jesus, His actions revealed that he doubted Him.

When we idolize security, we are tempted to keep our eyes on the external scenarios and potential dangers that linger, consequently taking our eyes off of Jesus. We are surrounded by things that threaten our security, and those things will not dissipate in this lifetime. Where we turn when our security is threatened reveals where our true faith lies. When we turn to ourselves, we may begin to build our lives around this idea that we have nothing to worry about as long as we have certain things keeping us secure. Our inclination is to fill our lives with things that feel strong, steady, and capable of weathering any circumstantial or unpredicted attack. We build up metaphorical walls that promise to protect us. But what we will eventually come to realize is that the walls of security we build for ourselves are flimsy and unreliable. Even if they withstand the weathering temporarily, they cannot withstand it forever.

When we turn to Jesus, we find a security that not only withstands this life but the life to come. Through salvation, we can boldly draw near to Him with a heart of full assurance and faith that He has promised to carry us through the uncertainties of life all the way to glory. This does not mean we will avoid trials and affliction. We will certainly be tempted and tried with situations we could never have imagined or predicted for ourselves. Satan wants nothing more than to use those situations to tempt us to doubt and to believe the lie that we are not really secure in Christ. He will coerce us in every way to look to other things on which to cling. But, enabled by the Holy Spirit, we are equipped to hold fast to Scripture to remind us to keep our eyes on Jesus, the pioneer and perfector of our faith. Not only does Jesus establish our security in Him through His life, death, and resurrection, but He sustains it. Even when Peter took his eyes off of Jesus, He was there to catch him and uphold him. It is Christ who holds us fast. He is constantly redirecting our hearts away from idolatry and toward Himself, reminding us of where we must look for true safety and security. May we pray for greater faith in Jesus, astounded by His faithfulness as He leads us safely by the hand through the wind and waves of life to arrive at eternity's shore.

Not only does Jesus establish our security in Him through His life, death, and resurrection, but He sustains it.

IN WHAT WAYS ARE YOU TEMPTED TO IDOLIZE SECURITY?

HOW MIGHT YOU, LIKE PETER, BE TEMPTED TO TAKE YOUR EYES OF JESUS WHEN THINGS FEEL UNSURE AND UNCERTAIN?

HOW DOES JESUS PROMISE GREATER SECURITY IN HIMSELF THAN THE WORLD COULD EVER OFFER?

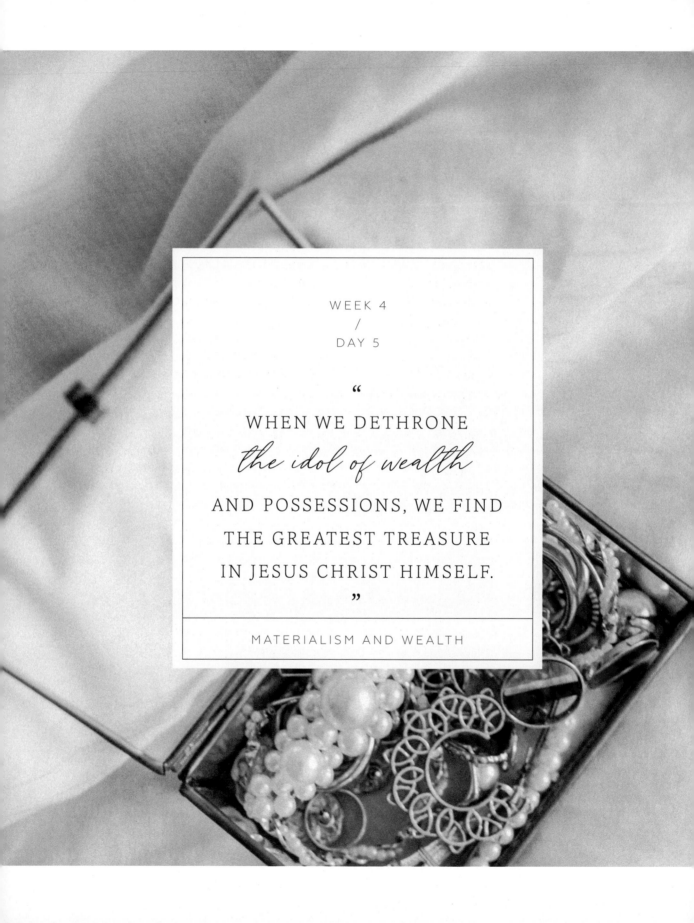

WEEK 4
/
DAY 5

"

WHEN WE DETHRONE
the idol of wealth
AND POSSESSIONS, WE FIND
THE GREATEST TREASURE
IN JESUS CHRIST HIMSELF.

"

MATERIALISM AND WEALTH

Materialism and Wealth

READ LUKE 18:18-30, MATTHEW 6:19-21

We are culturally indoctrinated with the desire to acquire. Advertisements are thoughtfully curated to make us feel like we need a certain product to make our lives better. Window displays help us to imagine ourselves in the newest outfits. Magazines showcase elaborate homes and luxurious cars. We convince ourselves of all the materialistic things we need to fill our lives with satisfaction. Consequently, the need for more things comes with a price tag. To have more things, we need to have more money, and therefore, the pursuit of wealth and materialism go hand in hand. We can feel the constant need for more things and more money. But the Bible reminds us of the dangers of being consumed by such desires.

From a societal standpoint, materialistic wealth is of great value and esteem. But how is it viewed by God? The parable of the rich, young ruler sheds light on materialism and wealth in the eyes of God. In Luke 18:18, Jesus encountered a wealthy young man who wanted to be accepted into God's kingdom and asked, "What must I do to inherit eternal life?" The young man felt he had honored and upheld the ten commandments, wondering if there was anything else he needed to do to be accepted by God. Even his best efforts at righteousness could never be enough. Exposing the young man's idolatry, Jesus responds, "You still lack one thing: sell all you have and distribute it to the poor, and you will have treasure in heaven. Then come, follow me" (Luke 18:22). The young man's response only affirmed evidence of the idol that prohibited him from fully following Jesus and inheriting eternal life. He became extremely sad because he was very rich, and he knew the cost would be great. Ultimately, when faced with the choice of his material possessions and his Savior, he chose his possessions. In what ways are we tempted to do the same?

We can use what we have been given to bless and serve others.

Materials and wealth are not inherently bad. Just like our success and achievements, we can use what we have been given to bless and serve others. Following Jesus does not mean we cannot accept a paycheck or purchase a new pair of jeans. God provides a way for us to appreciate and utilize them without making them a god. But idolizing our wealth and possessions can hinder us from surrendering everything to follow Jesus. Just like the rich young ruler, we may be more consumed by a love of things than of love for God. Our greatest pursuit becomes accumulating and storing up earthly treasures, regardless of the cost. But for what reason? Jesus implored the young man to give up anything that kept him from fully embracing Jesus with his whole heart. This instruction applies to us today. Jesus' perfect life, death, and resurrection provides the means for abundant riches and treasures to be received by those who inherit the kingdom of God (Matthew 13:44).

When we dethrone the idol of wealth and possessions, we find the greatest treasure in Jesus Christ Himself. No amount of possessions or wealth even compares to the riches found in a relationship with Jesus. Our stuff will never love us back, and our money will never secure a hope for us in the life to come, but Jesus will. We guard ourselves against the idol of wealth and materialism by holding all things loosely and offering all things back to the Lord to be used as He intends them to be used. We free ourselves up from the burden of acquiring more, and we open our hands to receive true and abundant riches offered to us in Christ.

Our stuff will never love us back, and our money will never secure a hope for us in the life to come, but Jesus will.

IN WHAT WAYS MIGHT YOU BE TEMPTED TO IDOLIZE WEALTH AND POSSESSIONS?

HOW DO WORLDLY TREASURES COMPARE TO ETERNAL TREASURES IN CHRIST? HOW CAN YOU INVEST IN THAT WHICH IS ETERNAL INSTEAD OF THAT WHICH IS TEMPORAL WITH YOUR WEALTH AND POSSESSIONS?

IN WHAT WAYS CAN WE GROW IN TREASURING OUR RELATIONSHIP WITH CHRIST MORE THAN ANYTHING ELSE?

It is FROM HIM that
you are in Christ Jesus,
who became wisdom
from God for us—our
righteousness, sanctification,
and redemption—in order
that, as it is written:
Let the one who boasts,
BOAST IN THE LORD.

1 Corinthians 1:30-31

WEEK 4 SCRIPTURE MEMORY

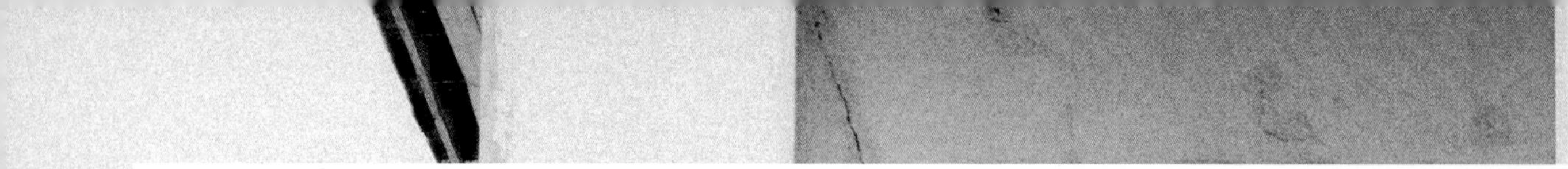

Week Four Reflection

review all passages from this week

Paraphrase the passages that stood out to you the most this week.

_____
_____
_____
_____
_____
_____
_____
_____
_____
_____

What did you observe from this week's text about God and His character?

_____
_____
_____
_____
_____
_____
_____
_____
_____
_____

What do these passages teach about the condition of mankind and about yourself?

_____
_____
_____
_____
_____
_____
_____
_____
_____
_____

How do these passages point to the gospel?

_____

_____

_____

_____

_____

How should you respond to these passages? What is the personal application?

_____

_____

_____

_____

_____

What specific action steps can you take this week to apply these passages?

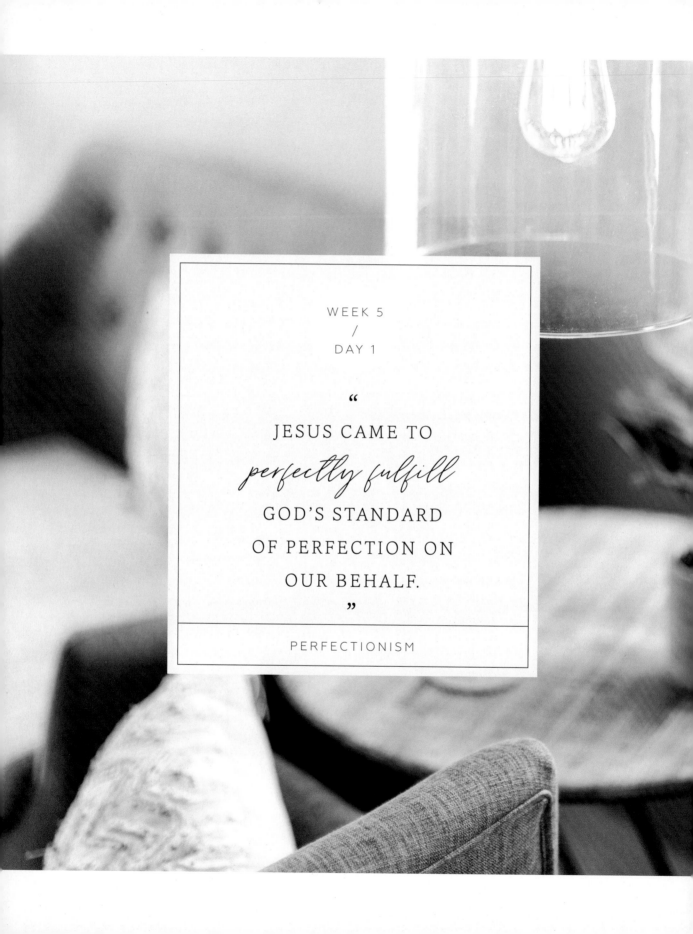

WEEK 5
/
DAY 1

"

JESUS CAME TO

perfectly fulfill

GOD'S STANDARD
OF PERFECTION ON
OUR BEHALF.

"

PERFECTIONISM

Perfectionism

READ ROMANS 5:7-8, ROMANS 3:23,
MATTHEW 11:28-30

Perfectionistic tendencies remain a common struggle for mankind. This is not to be mistaken for striving for virtue or excellence. Those are honorable things to pursue. The idol of perfectionism differs in that it aims to be without fault or flaw. It provides no room for shortcomings and growth and can leave us fixated obsessively on doing something perfect, or it can paralyze us from action in fear of failing. Idolizing perfectionism is most commonly rooted in pride or the fear of falling short. It can be easily reflected in the way someone deals with conflict, accidents, failures, or ruined plans. The way we respond to imperfect scenarios can reveal how much we cling to the idea of being perfect. Perfectionism may look different for everyone, but it remains a common struggle for mankind.

> *The way we respond to imperfect scenarios can reveal how much we cling to the idea of being perfect.*

Where does the idea of perfection stem from? First, we must understand that the Bible tells us there is a standard of perfection set for us. We may find this conflicting as we wrestle through the idol of perfectionism and the desire to be set free from it. Matthew 5:48 says, "Be perfect, therefore, as your heavenly Father is perfect." God does require perfection to have a right relationship with Him. At face value, this certainly sounds like a justification for perfectionism. However, Jesus made this statement in his Sermon on the Mount as a reiteration of how impossible it is by humanly standards to fulfill the standards of this law. This is inclusive of all of humanity. There is no human who can uphold the standard of perfection that was set by God because we have all sinned and fallen short of His glory.

Jesus prefaces His command to be perfect by saying, "Don't think I came to abolish the Law or the Prophets. I did not come to abolish but to fulfill" (Matthew 5:17). The demand of perfection remains, and our desire for it to be fulfilled is natural. But it cannot be fulfilled in ourselves. Jesus came to perfectly fulfill God's standard of perfection on our behalf. This resounding truth is reiterated in Hebrews 10:14, stating of Jesus, "For by one offering he has perfected forever those who are sanctified." He is the answer to our longing to be set free from this standard. Jesus perfectly meets it within Himself —through His perfect, sinless life.

In God's eyes, the standard of perfection is met for us through our salvific union with Christ. This does not leave God unaware of our sin and how it affects everything we do. But even in His all-inclusive knowledge of us, He chooses to see us perfectly righteous through Jesus Christ. This truth sets us free to be honest with others and ourselves about our imperfections. It sets us free from the exhausting maintenance of a perfect reputation. It sets us free to acknowledge our shortcomings through confession and repentance. It sets us free from the insecurity of being less than perfect. It sets us free to run with full abandon to the One who can give us rest from our attempts to be perfect. It sets us free to fight sin and embrace sanctification. Ultimately, it sets us free to live and engage imperfectly with a hope that lives outside of ourselves.

Though we battle daily with our imperfections, Jesus Christ is mending, molding, and shaping us to one day reflect His perfect nature. We are reminded that as He has begun the work of perfecting us, and He will bring it to full completion on the day of Christ Jesus. We no longer have to be enslaved by our own idolatrous pursuits. Instead, we can live in freedom, knowing that God is not looking for perfect behavior or perfect motives. Instead, He is looking for hearts that rest in the hope of Jesus, even if imperfectly, knowing that our longing for perfection is perfectly met and accomplished through Him.

Though we battle daily with our imperfections, Jesus Christ is mending, molding, and shaping us to one day reflect His perfect nature.

HOW ARE YOU TEMPTED TO IDOLIZE PERFECTION?

IN WHAT WAYS CAN WE LIVE IMPERFECTLY WHILE STILL FIGHTING SIN
AND EMBRACING SANCTIFICATION?

HOW DOES THE GOSPEL COMBAT OUR ATTEMPTS TO ACHIEVE PERFECTION?
HOW DOES JESUS MAKE A WAY FOR US TO MEET THE STANDARD OF
PERFECTION SET BY GOD?

WEEK 5
/
DAY 2

"

EVERY SOURCE OF

delight & joy

THAT WE FIND IN THINGS
OF THIS WORLD ARE
ULTIMATELY TO LEAD US
BACK TO THE SOURCE—GOD.

"

PLEASURE

Pleasure

READ 2 TIMOTHY 3:1-5, PSALM 16:11

Pleasure is the broad category of things that make us feel good. It is more of an experience that we seek after. God created us with senses to enjoy things, to delight in them, and to experience pleasure! Think of all the many things we find pleasure in—a warm cup of coffee, a good book, a delightful meal, a beautiful symphony, an extensive vacation, astounding architecture, or physical intimacy in marriage. When treasured as a gift given by God, pleasurable experiences can help sweeten our days and captivate our senses. But when treasured like a god, pleasurable experiences seduce and entice us into sin.

God created us with senses to enjoy things, to delight in them, and to experience pleasure!

We see the comparison in Scripture of those who are "lovers of pleasure rather than lovers of God" in Paul's letter to Timothy. The phrase, "lovers of pleasure," translates to the Greek word *philodonos*, which is a compound of two words, *phileo* and *hedonos*. The first word, *phileo*, conveys the ideas of affection and love. The word *hedonos* is used in Scripture to reference those preoccupied with pleasure and gratifying the desires of the flesh. Derived from *hedonas* is the term *Hedonism*, which encompasses the philosophical theory that pleasure is the highest good and proper aim of life. Humanity has wrestled with the temptation to idolize pleasure since the beginning of the fall, and the culmination of idolizing it is hedonism. It continually feeds the lie that we must pursue pleasure as the ultimate thing. However, in Paul's letter, he addresses the result of a life lived for pleasure. In the last days, he says those who lived for pleasure will be "lovers of self, lovers of money, boastful, proud, demeaning, disobedient to parents, ungrateful, unholy, unloving, irreconcilable, slanderers, without self-control, brutal, without love for what is good, traitors, reckless, conceited, lovers of pleasure rather than lovers of God, holding to the form of godliness but denying its power" (2 Timothy 3:2-5). It is evident that the promise of pleasure will lead to our own demise if we yield to its demand for our affections.

Pleasures are to be enjoyed within the confines of biblical principles. The beauty of God is that He provides all the pleasures of the world to be enjoyed by us, but He provides instruction and restraint to help us best enjoy them and protect us from idolatry. Money, sex, beauty, and experiences are pleasurable things to be enjoyed when we do so with proper regard to how Scripture calls us to use and appreciate them. Limitations provided to us in Scripture actually set us free to enjoy pleasures the way God intended us to. For example, sex is to be enjoyed within the confines of marriage. Wine is to be enjoyed in a way that does not lead to drunkenness. Food is to be enjoyed in a way that nourishes but does not turn us into gluttons. God is purposeful and intentional with His instruction because He knows the best way for these pleasures to be consumed for our good and His glory. When enjoyed outside of those bounds, we fall victim to temptation and sin. Pleasures enjoyed outside of biblical instruction lead to sexual immorality, drunkenness, greed, impurity, covetousness, and all kinds of reckless and lawless behavior. It feeds our fleshly desires for more and without restraint becomes idolatry and debauchery.

Giving ourselves to God's Word helps us to understand His instruction and equips us to fight against the sinful enticement of idolizing pleasure. Paul purposefully ends instruction to Timothy with a reminder of the power and sufficiency Scripture holds in our lives: "All Scripture is inspired by God and is profitable for teaching, for rebuking, for correcting, for training in righteousness, so that the man of God may be complete, equipped for every good work" (2 Timothy 3:16-17). We must rightly hold to God's Word in order to rightly enjoy the pleasures offered to us. We need it impressed in our hearts and minds to correct, direct, and equip us to enjoy pleasures in a godly way.

Every source of delight and joy that we find in things of this world are ultimately to lead us back to the source—God. As we are gifted with pleasures of this world, may we enjoy them in a way that leaves us longing for the giver, for at His right hand are pleasures forevermore.

It is evident that the promise of pleasure will lead to our own demise
if we yield to its demand for our affections.

HOW MIGHT YOU BE TEMPTED TO IDOLIZE PLEASURE?

IN WHAT WAYS DOES GOD'S WORD EQUIP US TO ENJOY PLEASURES OF THIS WORLD WITHOUT BEING CONSUMED BY THEM? HOW DO BIBLICAL LIMITATIONS SET US FREE TO ENJOY PLEASURES AS GOD INTENDED US TO?

HOW CAN ENJOYING PLEASURE ULTIMATELY LEAD US BACK TO GOD IN WORSHIP?

WEEK 5
/
DAY 3

"

GOD MUST REMAIN
THE RECIPIENT OF OUR
deepest praise &
greatest affection.

"

PASSIONS

Passions

READ PSALM 37:4, TITUS 3:3-7

Many of us have that one thing that ignites our creativity, fuels our imagination, or satisfies the need to express ourselves. For some of us, we find a passion for art, music, writing, making, or creating. Some find a passion for building, designing, gardening, baking, or teaching. Others find a passion for exploring, traveling, sporting, experiencing new things, learning new skills, or conquering new fears. The list could go on for things that kindle the fire of passion in our lives. Passions are anything that we strongly delight in with extravagant fondness. Passions often motivate us to act and engage as a means of expression. Passions can be hobbies, collections, skills, or interests. They can be a way to showcase our unique qualities and utilize our giftings. We can uniquely express ourselves through our passions. So how are we tempted to make an idol out of our passions?

God has gifted us with many wonderful gifts and graces for this lifetime to be celebrated and enjoyed.

Over the course of this study, we may be continually surprised by the things that fight for our affections. God has gifted us with many wonderful gifts and graces for this lifetime to be celebrated and enjoyed. But due to our fallen nature, we can easily blur the line between a gift and a god. Our passions are intended to draw our hearts back to the giver of such good gifts. They are meant to leave us in awe of who God is and how He has created us to live and reflect Him. But even with godly intentions for our passions, we can become consumed by them. We can look to them to fulfill our hearts desires and give us meaning and purpose. The manifestation of idolizing our passions looks like finding our identity in those things. It looks like needing passion-filled experiences to feel meaning and direction in our life. It looks like exhausting our resources, our time, and our energy to satisfy our passions. It looks like loving our passions more than we love God. Our lives will reflect where our heart truly lies and what we love the most. What do our passions say about us? Are we more passionate about God or something else? Do we use our passions to glorify God or ourselves? Our passions must continually be assessed through that lens. God must remain the recipient of our deepest praise and greatest affection. This does not mean we must be passionless. But it does mean that our passions must be saturated with the desire to love God with all of our heart, mind, soul, and strength.

The beauty of expressing our passions is that we are able to reflect our passionate Savior. His greatest interest and desire was to reconcile God's people back to Himself so that God would be glorified, and His people could be satisfied. He did so through a passionate display of love and sacrifice on the cross. He found His greatest delight in accomplishing the will of the Father by offering salvation to all who would place their hope and faith in Him. He modeled perfectly for us what our ultimate aim and pursuit in life must be. We can explore our passions, while still giving the glory where it is due. We can delight in the giftings, craftsmanship, and aspirations God has given us without worshiping them. We can express our interests and eager longings, while reflecting God's creative and wonder-filled nature. We can be eager and willing to pursue our passions, while ultimately yearning to be with the One who gives us purpose and identity.

We can be eager and willing to pursue our passions, while ultimately yearning to be with the One who gives us purpose and identity.

HOW MIGHT YOU BE TEMPTED TO IDOLIZE YOUR PASSIONS?

HOW CAN WE EXPLORE OUR PASSIONS WITHOUT FINDING OUR
PURPOSE AND IDENTITY IN IT?

IN WHAT WAYS CAN YOU USE YOUR SPECIFIC PASSIONS TO THE GLORY OF GOD?

WEEK 5
/
DAY 4

"

THOUGH CREATED TO
SERVE AND HELP US,

*screens can easily
enslave us.*

"

SCREENS

Screens

READ ROMANS 12:2, PHILIPPIANS 4:8,
1 CORINTHIANS 6:12

There are a million small and big ways that our lives have been transformed by screens. From the moment phones, television, and computers entered into society, our lives were changed. It is impossible to ignore the impact screens have had in our world and in our lives. They inform the way we speak, relate, act, think, and live. They contribute to our worldview. They connect us to people and places all over the globe. We are able to accomplish the most difficult things with a click of a button. We have access to a wealth of information just through a search engine. We can get places we need to go. We can ask the questions we need answered. We are even provided a source of entertainment. The ever-evolving world of screens can benefit and add to our lives tremendously, but we must also remain cognizant of the equal amount of dangers. Though created to serve and help us, screens can easily enslave us.

From the moment phones, television, and computers entered into society, our lives were changed.

Do we run to our screens first thing in the morning? Do we look at them in idle time? Do our screens push time with God to the margins? Do we find ourselves unwilling to be without them? These questions can serve as a probe for identifying whether we worship our screens. We can be consumed by our phones, computers, and television in a number of ways. We can use them to connect with others in a way that dictates and rules our time and attention. We can use them to search for approval and recognition through social media platforms. We can use them to groom lustful thoughts or view pornography. We can use them to indulge in sports, news, and pop culture in a way that encourages sinful thoughts. We can use the mindless entertainment they provide as a source of relief to our stress.

Not only can our screen be idols, but they can also be an enabler of other idols. With access to so much, screens can be a vehicle to engage in other forms of misplaced worship. They can provide numerous opportunities to engage in additional things we struggle with. If we wrestle with idolizing materialism and wealth, we may be more tempted through advertisements and promotions to find the newest and greatest thing to splurge on. If we struggle with idolizing appearance, we may find ourselves curating deceptive social media posts. If we struggle with idolizing marriage, we may find ourselves discontent and frustrated by the marriages we see displayed on television. These are only a few examples, but it remains clear that temptation lurks, and we must be careful with how we use our screens.

Battling the idolatry of screens, like many good things provided to us, must come with intentionality and thoughtfulness about how we use them. Movies and television shows can entertain us, and sometimes the story lines can even redemptively point us back to the gospel. News channels, websites, and podcasts can inform us, help us understand the world around us, and stir us to action. Social media can connect us to people all over the world and provide us a platform to share our lives and learn from one another. To fight the temptation to be enslaved by our screens, we must set proper boundaries and limitations. We can set a limit to the time we will engage with our screens. We can be careful about what we will watch on television and consider the value it adds to our time. We can be conscious about our motivations with social media platforms by being careful of who we follow, what we post, and when we are just mindlessly scrolling. We can think about how our screens are feeding and forming our thoughts. Everything we do can either help us or hurt us. There are so many ways our screens can be of benefit to us and our lives. Our hope as we engage with them is to hold them loosely with the highest regard to how the gospel informs and shapes us. With minds and hearts transformed by the work of the gospel, we can properly engage with our screens in a godly way.

Battling the idolatry of screens, like many good things provided to us, must come with intentionality and thoughtfulness about how we use them.

QUESTIONS

HOW MIGHT YOU BE TEMPTED TO IDOLIZE YOUR SCREENS?

IN WHAT WAYS CAN WE SINFULLY ENGAGE WITH OUR SCREENS? IN WHAT WAYS CAN WE ENGAGE WITH THEM IN A GODLY WAY?

HOW DOES THE GOSPEL TRANSFORM THE WAY WE UTILIZE OUR SCREENS?

WEEK 5
/
DAY 5

"

OUR GREATEST HOPE FOR
TURNING FROM IDOLATRY
IS LOVING GOD

*more than
anything else.*

"

TURNING FROM IDOLS

Turning from Idols: Loving God More Than Anything

READ MATTHEW 22:37, PHILIPPIANS 3:8

We have addressed a number of potential idols that we may struggle with in our lives. But even the content provided in this study is not exhaustive. You may think of other ways you are tempted to misdirect your worship toward something other than God, and it is important that you assess and explore those temptations. As we continue on in the journey of faith, we will be tempted and tried by many things that contend for our worship. But we can be assured that regardless of what seeks after our affections, we are equipped in every way to turn from idols. As we have addressed specific ways for the idols listed in this study, there are a few general ways to think preventatively and practically about dethroning our idols.

> *We can be assured that regardless of what seeks after our affections,*
> *we are equipped in every way to turn from idols.*

Ultimately, the Holy Spirit must convict us in our idolatry. We will not always be able to see ourselves clearly, and we need the work of the Spirit in our hearts to expose us in our idolatrous ways. This is the transforming work of the gospel. With the help of the Spirit, our blind eyes are continually unveiled to see the reality of our sin and sanctified to see the righteousness of God. We can regularly pray and ask God to point out any misplaced worship in our lives, to convict us, and to uncover the hidden motives of our heart no matter the cost.

As God reveals the true desires of our hearts, we must identify what misbelief about God ultimately resulted in idolatry and combat it with the truth of Scripture. God's Word is living and active, discerning, and pierces the lies that seek to entangle us. It serves as an armor of protection, helping us stand on guard against the temptations and schemes of Satan that entice us to worship something other than God. It provides instruction, guidance, and truth for us to be wise and discerning in the way we engage with the world. It also helps us to know God more and cultivate a love for Him that surpasses our love for everything else.

Additionally, we must surround ourselves with godly people who will lovingly and truthfully redirect us. Often our greatest moments of weakness are enhanced in isolation or when no one knows the temptations we face. We are safeguarded when we confess and share our vulnerabilities and struggles with others. They are able to pray for us, share our burdens, and help us fight against any idolatrous way in us. God is purposeful in providing us with community. We are wise to share in the accountability and encouragement offered to us through it.

As we think about proper worship, we must realize that worship does not only happen on Sundays or while reading the Bible. Worship happens when we take notice of God's grand and glorious attributes, when we praise and thank Him for His good gifts, and when we acknowledge His hand in all things. We must display active worship in our hearts and lives. Continually acknowledging His righteous rule and reign in our hearts leaves no room for idolatry. Our worship becomes God-centered. He must receive all the glory and honor and praise that our hearts have to offer. A deep and devoted worship of Him is cultivated out of a deep love for Him. Our greatest hope for turning from idolatry is loving God more than anything else. He is the one who fulfills our every longing. He is the one who satisfies our every need. He is the one who gives us purpose in this life. He is the one who keeps His promises. He is the one who sustains us from birth to the death. What other god could contend? None. May we long for no one else, nothing else, but God, and may He prove time and time again why He is more worthy of our worship than anything else. Assuredly, He will.

He must receive all the glory and honor and praise that our hearts have to offer.

HOW HAS YOUR UNDERSTANDING OF IDOLATRY BEEN SHAPED
AND TRANSFORMED BY THIS STUDY?

WHAT PRACTICAL WAYS DO YOU FIND HELPFUL FOR THE FIGHT AGAINST IDOLATRY?
WHAT AREA DO YOU MOST LACK IN HELPING YOU FIGHT AGAINST IDOLATRY?

HOW CAN YOU CONSIDER YOUR WORSHIP OF GOD IN YOUR EVERYDAY LIFE?

HOW CAN YOUR LIFE REFLECT THAT YOU LOVE GOD MORE THAN ANYTHING?

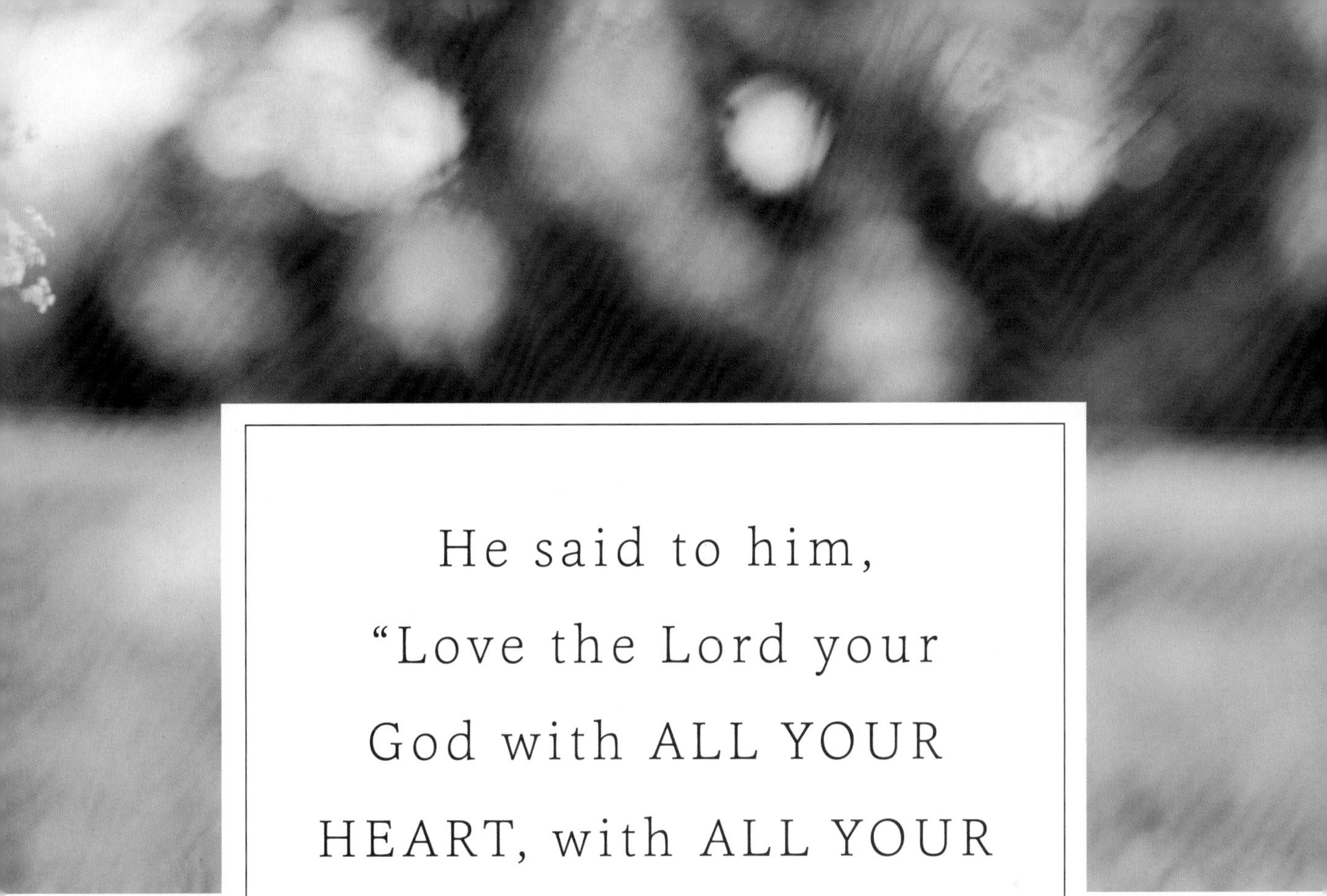

He said to him,
"Love the Lord your
God with ALL YOUR
HEART, with ALL YOUR
SOUL, and with ALL
YOUR MIND."

Matthew 22:37

WEEK 5 SCRIPTURE MEMORY

Week Five Reflection

review all passages from this week

Paraphrase the passages that stood out to you the most this week.

_____
_____
_____
_____
_____
_____
_____
_____
_____
_____

What did you observe from this week's text about God and His character?

_____
_____
_____
_____
_____
_____
_____
_____
_____

What do these passages teach about the condition of mankind and about yourself?

_____
_____
_____
_____
_____
_____
_____
_____
_____

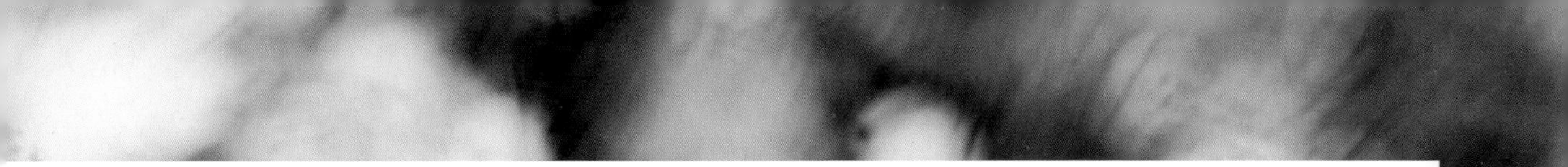

How do these passages point to the gospel?

_____

_____

_____

_____

_____

_____

How should you respond to these passages? What is the personal application?

_____

_____

_____

_____

_____

_____

What specific action steps can you take this week to apply these passages?

Idolatry Diagnostics

An extensive list of diagnostic questions is provided to help you think through potential idols in your life. As you read through each question, consider the things that are recurring answers and how you might be tempted toward idolatry.

(1) WHAT HAVE I BEEN WILLING TO COMMIT SIN OVER IN ORDER TO OBTAIN? WHAT HAVE I BEEN WILLING TO SIN OVER IF I DO NOT GET IT?

(2) WHAT MUST I POSSESS TO BE HAPPY? WHAT BRINGS ME ULTIMATE JOY?

(3) WHAT DO I FEEL LIKE I TRULY NEED?

(4) WHAT DEMANDS MY TIME?

(5) WHAT CONSUMES MY THOUGHTS? WHAT DO I THINK OF FIRST THING IN THE MORNING? WHAT CONTROLS OR RULES ME?

(6) WHAT MAKES MY EMOTIONS UNCONTROLLABLE?

(7) WHAT BRINGS ME THE GREATEST PEACE AND CONTENTMENT?

(8) WHAT MAKES MY LIFE FEEL PURPOSEFUL AND MEANINGFUL?

(13) WHOSE LOVE AND APPROVAL DO I NEED THE MOST?

(9) WHAT DO I MOST PRAY FOR? WHAT UNANSWERED PRAYERS MAKE ME ANGRY OR DISAPPOINTED?

(14) WHERE DO I FIND MY IDENTITY?

(15) WHERE DO I PLACE MY HOPE?

(10) WHAT DO I RUN TO FOR COMFORT? HOW DO I RELIEVE STRESS OR PRESSURE IN MY LIFE?

(16) WHAT MOTIVATES ME?

(11) WHAT IS MY GREATEST AIM AND PURSUIT IN LIFE? WHAT ARE MY PLANS, AGENDAS, STRATEGIES, AND INTENTIONS DESIGNED TO ACCOMPLISH?

(17) WHAT DO I CRAVE AND LONG FOR? WHAT IS THE DEEPEST DESIRE OF MY HEART?

(12) WHAT AM I MOST AFRAID OF?

Idols of the Heart

Worship is an overflow of what we believe in our hearts. The worship of idols is born out of a misbelief about who God is. When we believe lies about God, we open the door to direct our hearts to other things.

BELIEF ABOUT GOD ⟵   ⟶ MISBELIEF ABOUT GOD

I trust in Him to meet my deepest needs.	I do not trust in Him to meet my deepest needs.
I find my identity and purpose in Him.	He does not give me identity and purpose, but other things will.
I find no good thing apart from Him.	He is withholding good things from me.
He is the only one who can truly fulfill my every longing.	I can find fulfillment in other things.
He is worthy of my deepest praise and worship.	I can make a better god for myself.

WHAT WE BELIEVE ABOUT GOD WILL BE
DISPLAYED IN WHAT WE WORSHIP.

EXALT GOD

We worship as we were created to worship, and we find true purpose, security, and fulfillment in our Creator, God.

We enjoy creation without idolizing it. Even in the uncertain and unknown, we trust in His ultimate provision and care.

EXALT IDOLS

We worship the created rather than the Creator, and we find that nothing of this world can truly give us the purpose, security or fulfillment we long for.

Our idols will fail us in every way and leave us longing for the only one worthy of our worship.

We cultivate what we believe to be true about God by clinging to His Word. We fight unbelief by remembering His attributes, His character, and every way He has cared for and provided for us.

Heart Diagnostics

After completing this study, take a personal look at the underlying beliefs in your heart about God that tempt you to turn to idols.

(1) WHAT ARE YOU MOST TEMPTED TO IDOLIZE? LIST UP TO FIVE THINGS (REFERENCE IDOLATRY DIAGNOSTICS).

(2) WHAT MISBELIEF ABOUT GOD LEADS YOU TO TURN TO THESE IDOLS?

(3) IN WHAT WAYS HAVE THESE IDOLS LED YOU TO SIN?

(4) WHAT DOES REPENTING OF IDOLATRY AND TURNING FROM THESE IDOLS LOOK LIKE?

(5) WHAT TRUTH ABOUT GOD REFUTES YOUR INITIAL UNBELIEF? FIND SCRIPTURE TO SUPPORT YOUR ANSWER.

(6) HOW DO THESE TRUTHS ABOUT GOD DRAW YOU CLOSER TO HIM?

(7) HOW CAN YOU LIVE OUT THESE TRUTHS IN A WAY THAT COMBATS THE TEMPTATION TO MISPLACE YOUR WORSHIP FOR ANYTHING OTHER THAN GOD? HOW CAN THESE TRUTHS LEAD YOU TO LOVE GOD MORE THAN ANYTHING ELSE?

Post Study Prayer

Heavenly Father,

I come before You with an honest assessment of my limitations.

I know my heart wanders and that I am tempted to love
other things more than You.

I am tempted to doubt You and question You.

I am tempted to believe lies that You withhold good things from me.

I am tempted to believe You will not provide and care for me.

I am tempted to search for my identity and purpose in other things.

I am tempted to become impatient and discontent with Your timing.

I am tempted to believe that I can make a better god for myself.

I am tempted to believe that created things will satisfy and
fulfill me more than You, the Creator.

—

Lord, continually convict me of my idolatrous ways.

Leave me discontent and dissatisfied when misplacing
my worship to anything other than You.

Open my eyes to see that nothing of this world will satisfy my needs and
fulfill my every longing like You will.

Expose the sinful inclinations of my heart and any wicked desire in me.

Turn my eyes from being enticed and consumed by the things of this world.

Use my failings and shortcomings to draw me closer to You.

Use my weakness to remind me of Your strength.

I praise You for Your compassionate love toward me.

Even when I fail You, You never fail me.

You search me out and pursue me.

You were willing to send Your only Son to rescue me, to sacrifice
His life for me, and to reunite me to You.

You have given me abundant joy and eternal life through Jesus.

Every good thing is found in You.

You deserve all my honor and worship and praise.

—

Help me to delight in the riches and instruction of Your Word.

Surround me with those who will lovingly and truthfully
point me back to You.

Help me to lead a life of intentional, heartfelt worship unto You.

Deepen my understanding and delight in You.

Help my unbelief.

Remind me of the worthlessness of idols.

Equip me in every way to fight them.

Lead me to love You more than anything else.

Amen

Thank you for studying
God's Word with us!

CONNECT WITH US

@thedailygraceco

@kristinschmucker

CONTACT US

info@thedailygraceco.com

SHARE

#thedailygraceco

#lampandlight

VISIT US ONLINE

thedailygraceco.com

MORE DAILY GRACE

The Daily Grace App
Daily Grace Podcast